92 Acharnon Street

JOHN LUCAS

ELAND
London

First published by Eland Publishing Limited
61 Exmouth Market, London EC1R 4QL in 2007
This paperback edition published in 2011

Text © John Lucas
ISBN 978 1 906011 57 4

Cover designed by Katy Kedward
Cover Image: *George drinking local wine* © Pamela Browne

Text set by Katy Kedward
Printed in Navarra, Spain by GraphyCems

92 Acharnon Street

For my grandchildren,
Amanda, Sam, and Macayla

'Possess, as I possessed a season,
The countries I resign'
A E Housman

Contents

Illustrations

The publishers would like to thank Pamela Browne for permission to reproduce her photographs here. They were all shot in Athens in the late '70s and early '80s, either on assignment or as a *flâneur*. This is the first time that these images have been published.

'Other countries may offer you discoveries in manners or love or landscape; Greece offers you something harder – the discovery of yourself.'

Lawrence Durrell, *Prospero's Cell*

Introduction

TWO THOUSAND years ago, the poet Ovid was banished from Rome for upsetting Augustus Caesar. Quite what he had done to displease his emperor remains obscure, though the likeliest explanation is that something in *Ars Amatoria* prompted the imperial edict. Whatever the cause, Ovid was banished to Tomis on the west bank of the Black Sea. From there, in shock and bitter disappointment, he wrote his *Tristia*, describing the tedious years of exile and his boredom in an uncouth land. But if he hoped that this would soften Augustus's obduracy, he was wrong. He was still in exile when he died, in AD18. Nothing he said could change Augustus' mind, not even the claim that he, Ovid, was a Roman through and through and that, while you could change the skies under which a man lived, you couldn't change his soul.

I was forty-seven years old when, in August 1984, I began a year of living in Athens. From early adulthood I'd wanted to go to Greece, but for a variety of reasons every plan fell through, and during the infamous period of the colonels' junta (1967-74) visiting the country was simply not an option. Then, early in 1984, came an invitation to spend the academic year 1984-5 as visiting professor in the English department at the University of Athens. The details of how this came about and its consequences I leave until later. Here, I want to say only that the twelve months I spent living in Athens, while they may not radically have changed me, uncovered possibilities which, but for that year, might have remained hidden.

This is by no means to say that I approved of everything I found there. Bureaucracy, of which I encountered all too much, was, as it remains, a nightmare. Nothing was ever done as and when it should have been. Half the time you couldn't even locate the official who was supposed to deal with whatever case you were required to present to him. Either you had just missed him or he would be in tomorrow. (Oh, no, he wouldn't.) And if you did track him down, he would tell you that you had the wrong documentation. 'But this is what I was told to bring.' A dismissive shrug. 'You must apply to Mr X.' 'But Mr X told me I must apply to you.' A further shrug.

Much later, the poet and translator, Philip Ramp, tried to explain Greek bureaucracy to me. Philip and his wife Sarah, Americans who came to Greece in the late 1960s, are long-term residents on the island of Aegina, where my wife and I now have a small rented flat, and over the years we've become good friends. As well as making excellent translations of Greek poets, Philip has done much bread-and-butter work for Greek officialdom. He therefore knows more than most about the ways of the nation's bureaucracy, and has no doubt as to why it is so uniquely awful. 'In every other country', Phil says, 'bureaucrats are likely to be soulless, but after all they're not paid to have souls. They're paid to be efficient. And for the most part they are. You may not like them but they get the job done. They take pride in their work. But in Greece, nobody wants to be a bureaucrat. You go to see one and he's not interested in discussing the reason you're there. He wants to talk to you about poetry or art or music. And you know what, he's almost certain to have a slim volume in his bottom drawer just waiting for a publisher. He'll be OK as long as you keep to every subject but the one you came to him about, but as for the goddam money you're owed by his department, or the piece of paper you need to get some work done, forget it.'

That Philip is right about this, I discovered not merely from my own experiences but from a tale told to me by the artist, Andreas Foukas. Just after he had gone to live on Aegina, Andreas took his car down to the port, left it while he did some shopping, and when he came back found he had been ticketed for illegal parking. Given that the police of Aegina are hardly ever to be spotted on the streets (although you can sometimes glimpse them at a waterfront *ouzerie*), this was a rare piece of bad luck. However, seeing the policeman nearby who had, he assumed, issued the ticket, Andreas went up to him and, as is the Greek way, began a lengthy explanation, amounting to an apologia, not to say exculpation, as to why he'd parked in the wrong place, stressing the fact that he was new to the island and that he would be certain not to transgress a second time. He also took care to lob in some compliments to the island and to its officials, including, naturally enough, its police force. After about twenty minutes of this the policeman tore up the parking ticket, and the two men, having shaken hands, went their separate ways.

Two weeks later Andreas drove down to the port town, parked in exactly the same spot and, when he returned from his shopping, found the same policeman waiting for him. This time there was to be no reprieve. Andreas had gone back on his word and now he was for it. Well, perhaps he could plead his case with the inspector? You can try, the now less-than-friendly policeman told him, but you will not succeed. He marched Andreas to the police station, where they found the inspector (asleep at his desk, so Andreas told me), the policeman reported Andreas's two transgressions, and Andreas was then left to confront the inspector. As the policeman had forewarned, the inspector was not a man to be trifled with. Illegal parking was a most heinous crime and punishment would be exacted. Why, anyway, had Andreas dared to repeat the offence?

'I was in search of canvas and paint.'

'You are an artist?'

Yes, Andreas said, he was an artist.

A pause. The inspector, it transpired, was himself an artist. He would value Andreas's opinion of a small water-colour he had recently finished and which he happened to have with him. The painting was produced, Andreas offered his professional judgement, much talk on subjects relating to art followed, and at the end of an hour the inspector and Andreas shook hands.

'And my parking ticket?' Andreas asked, as he made for the door.

'Please to give it here.' The ticket was torn in half and dropped into the waste paper basket.

I told this story to another Greek friend, George the hairdresser, who also lives on the island. For thirty years George made his money by cutting hair in High Wycombe, and then, with money he had carefully saved, he and his wife Nikki, both originally from Cyprus, came to Aegina and built a house there. Not long after we had got to know them, and when the house was gleamingly new, we were invited to look it over. In the living-room I noticed a framed letter from a royal hanger-on of the house of Windsor, thanking George for his poem on the birth of Charles and Diana's first son. So George was a poet? Occasionally, he said, but it was not a major preoccupation. When he was not cutting islanders' hair, or acting as guide to anyone who wanted to visit the dormant volcano on Methena (which faces across to Aegina from the mainland), or tending the gardens of the newly finished, ambitious monastery of Nektarios in the middle of the island, or helping out on his brother's fruit farm on the far side of Aegina, or doing a thousand and one other things, he liked to fill his spare time by building model boats. When he told me about this I at first thought he meant ships in bottles. But then he took us to see them. I could hardly have been more wrong. Over the years George has constructed some forty large-scale models of boats that between them comprise a history of Greek maritime life, from ships that sailed to destroy Troy's topless towers, through trading vessels of the classical period, Phoenician and Roman as well as Greek, to latter-day merchant ships. And not merely the vessels themselves. There are lovingly-made model cranes, blocks-and-tackle, bales, boxes, men and pack animals at work. For a while George set up a small museum – in fact a vacant shop – in Agia Marina, the unattractive pleasure-town on the far side of the island, but then a sudden and wholly unreasonable tax demand forced him out. For him island bureaucracy is a nightmare from which it is impossible to wake. Now the ships are kept in the basement of a second house he's built at Alones (the word means 'threshing floor'), a village not far from Agia Marina, and he shows people his exhibition for free, talking them through Greek history as he does so, especially the history of Greek seafaring. It isn't what you'd expect of an English hairdresser. It is, though, what I have come to expect of many Greeks I know.

There is a kind of know-how/can-do that is taken for granted among them. This doesn't always bode well. On more than one occasion I have come to grief over a friend who claimed to be able to solve any plumbing or electrical problem I presented him with. And it's all but impossible to convince someone of the error of his ways. He is right, but right in a different way from the way you wanted. And his is the *right* right way. Philip gave me a hair-raising example of this insistence on infallibility. Some years ago a mainlander bought a plot of land near the foot of the island which had a spectacular view over the Saronic Gulf. He then hired an architect to draw up plans for a house he wanted built on the land he'd acquired, with windows looking out over the sea. A local builder engaged to have the house ready within twelve months and, having handed over a good deal of money, the man went back to Athens, safe in the knowledge that his house would be ready for him when he returned. Twelve months later he returned to the island. The house was ready and waiting. There was, however, a problem. Not a single window faced the sea. Instead, and without exception, each confronted a singularly drab piece of scrubland. And it wasn't just the windows. Porch, patio, upstairs veranda, all faced the same way and that way was inland. The builder was sent for. Why on earth had he entirely ignored the architect's plans? Why, oh, why had the house turned its back on the view its owner coveted? The builder shrugged. 'I thought it looked better that way round,' he said.

A refusal to follow approved or orthodox procedure was, I soon came to understand, commonplace, and could be infuriating. But it was the price to be paid for something I grew to love: a deep-rooted sense that individual lives are of paramount importance and not to be held to account by, let alone made the victim of, some god almighty officialdom. When I arrived in Athens in August 1984 I left behind me a nation that was growing increasingly cowed by such officialdom. One reason why the miners' strike, which had just begun, found supporters even among those who might have been expected at the very least to look the other way, was that it embodied a protest against a new, particularly nasty element in British politics, or at least one that in post-war years hadn't previously dared to show itself. The miners weren't after all striking for more money or even better conditions. They were striking for the right to work. They were striking on behalf of what was still called the Dignity of Labour. And they were opposed by a set of men, and a woman, for whom such dignity meant less than nothing. Parkinson, Tebbitt, Baker, Clarke, Heseltine, Howe, and above all Thatcher were at one in their jeering contempt for the miners' cause.

Nor were they alone. By 1984 something pretty horrible had begun to infect public life in Britain. You could smell its presence in the very language used by politicians, by business executives, by educational administrators. It was the language of sadism masquerading as masochism. It was about pain. 'We must take some painful managerial decisions' – meaning, *we're* going to sack *you*. 'It is time to bite the bullet' – meaning, *we're* the sawbones who will cut off *your* employment. 'We must grasp the nettle' – meaning, *you're* the one who will be stung. And all of this was in the interest of being 'leaner and fitter'. Down with isomorphs, away with endomorphs, from now on the world was to be made safe for mesomorphs. It can hardly be coincidence that this was precisely the moment when health clubs began springing up all over the place, where newly lean and fit executives and their epigoni were to be found pumping iron, burning rubber, and generally presenting hawk-like and 'accosting profiles' to the world. (Note the washboard stomach, the packed pectorals.) Nor can it be coincidence that this was the moment of 'nouvelle cuisine' – pay more, eat less – nor that those who knelt at the altar of the new orthodoxy tended to wear the 'executive' shirt that was suddenly all the rage. This was a shirt whose collar and cuffs were white, although the body of the shirt came in gamey reds, blues, or greens. See, I'm a sporty type, the shirt said, but I'm serious, too. More menacingly, it said, I may look like fun but don't try messing with me. 'What kind of prat wears a shirt like that?' a friend asked in desperate, cod rhyme. Answer: the kind of prat perfectly happy to sack a few hundred men before settling down to a fruit juice and a slice of rye bread (unbuttered).

I don't remember ever coming across such a shirt in Athens. I do remember, however, asking myself how many men it took to give you a piece of bread. In Babi's taverna, my favourite eating place and a place to whose joys I devote a chapter, the answer was three. One to cut the bread, one to put the slices into a basket, and one to bring the basket to your table. I don't imagine Babi gave any of them much if any money, but they all got fed, and customers' tips would no doubt be shared among them. A shirt would have got rid of them without delay. Yes, but the rule of shirts didn't operate in Babi's taverna. Nor, as far as I could see, did it operate anywhere in Greece, not successfully, anyway. A change of skies indeed. And a change of soul? The pages that follow may provide an answer to that question.

Athens in Summer

'Sweet hour. Athens reclines and gives herself
To April like a beauteous courtesan'
KOSTAS KARIOTAKIS

And at six o'clock this late, gamey August,
she sprawls under a blanket of sun, sweat
rankled with petrol fumes, cheap deodorants, dust:
everywhere litters of taxis squeal and fret
and root out fare among herds of lowing cars.

On a silver pool of café tables, pale
clouds of ouzo settle, milkily calm
as love achieved. Then daylight blows a fuse
and night swarms down the flats' high cliff edges
past balconies where lamps suddenly fruit.

A teeming, seedy city, she feeds and farms
most present hungers, vine-roofed tavernas bale-
high with student politicos' yelp and bark.
Attica's pillars are lost in the sky's soot
where all the streets ride on under the dark.

CHAPTER ONE

92 Acharnon Street

GEORGE PHONED one evening in May. 'John, I have found you a flat. It is near where I myself live, and I may say that it will do very well. It is…' At this point his voice was submerged under a series of howls and clicks. When the line cleared George wanted to know what had happened.

'We're probably being bugged,' I said.

George was indignant. 'That is not possible. Greece is a free country.'

'Lucky you,' I said. The bugging, if that's what it was, was in all probability at our end. It was early summer, 1984, both Pauline and I worked for CND and were helping to run a support group for the striking miners; and Thatcher had given public approval to police and MI5 tactics for keeping tabs on anybody 'not one of us'.

I explained this – no harm in letting the listeners know you're onto them – but George was by now talking over my words. The flat had two bedrooms, lounge, bathroom, 'and a proper kitchen'.

'Sounds ideal,' I said.

George was suddenly cautious. 'I hope you will not be disappointed.'

'I'm sure I won't be,' I told him. We said our goodbyes, and feeling mightily relieved at the prospect of a roof over my head for when I got to Athens, I put the phone down.

Three months earlier I had received, quite unexpectedly, a letter from the University of Athens, inviting me to spend a year there as Visiting Professor. (Lord Byron Visiting Professor of English Literature was, I think, the full title, and as I was to discover, the glory was all in that title.) I was both flattered and excited. But would my own university give me a year's leave of absence? Yes, they would.

So I wrote back to Athens saying that I'd be delighted to take up the invitation and asking for details of the appointment. No administration was involved, I was assured, and I would only be required to teach one course. Given that whatever reputation I enjoyed in academic circles had been acquired for a series of studies on nineteenth-century literature, especially Dickens, I assumed that the course would be on a subject related to my 'specialism'.

Well, no. Professor R, head of English Studies, explained that he had a full complement of staff to teach the nineteenth century. However, he and his advisors would appreciate my offering a course on Shakespeare's major plays. Puzzled, but not greatly put out – who after all wouldn't relish the chance to throw in his tuppence worth on *Romeo and Juliet, Measure for Measure, Hamlet, Lear*, and *The Tempest*? – I went along with the request.

Good. And would I please send details about my date of birth, education, including degrees, major publications, academic career? Professor R would then at once complete the paperwork that would enable me to be put on the payroll as soon as I arrived in Athens. He closed by asking whether he could be of assistance in finding me suitable accommodation. 'No,' I told him, many thanks but I already had someone on the case.

A while earlier, by one of life's great coincidences, a Mr George Dandoulakis had written to me from Athens, where he taught English at the Military Academy, asking whether I might be interested in supervising a doctoral thesis he proposed to write on the poetry of the Greek Liberation. Intrigued, but far from certain I was the right person to oversee such work, I suggested that he might like to come to Loughborough to discuss his proposal. And so, on a hot day in June 1982, George and I met for the first time.

I hope he won't mind me saying that he looked far from comfortable in the heavy tweed suit he presumably thought appropriate to the occasion, wrapped tightly round his thickset body as it was, and his discomfort was increased by the lunchtime trout we were served at the University club, fish he'd never seen before, and which couldn't be attacked in the Greek way. For one thing, it had more bones than he was used to, as an experimental mouthful made plain. And which pieces of cutlery were you supposed to use? It was seeing George hesitate at the bewildering choice of knives and forks placed before him that sharpened my sense of how cutlery is part of the world of conspicuous consumption, and how bloody daft we are to be cowed into thinking that a table isn't properly laid until there are rows of silverware gleaming like surgical tools on each side of the place mat. Veblen was right. Who on earth needs fish knives and forks? Not George for sure. I think that meal must have been one of the few in his life from which he rose hungry.

No matter. I liked him, liked his ruddy-faced, round-eyed expression of watchful good cheer, the mobility of a look that could in an instant change from solemnity to laughter. Over coffee, we talked about his proposal, and I said that insofar as it involved English poets, pre-eminently Byron and Shelley, I'd feel confident that I could help him. The Greek poets, though, were a different kettle of fish. I knew nothing of importance about either Solomos or Kalvos, the two poets he would have to bring into his thesis. What to suggest? As far as I recall, we left it that I would make enquiries about possible extra supervision on the Greek writers. In the meantime, he might like to write a chapter outlining the years leading up to the War of Independence, and including any relevant material on poetic works of the time. Then we could take stock, and if either felt uneasy with the other, we could agree to part company before getting too deeply involved. Agreed? Agreed.

Over the following months work began to arrive, written out in painstaking longhand, and each new piece made me the more certain that this was a man who meant business. Then came the letter from the University of Athens. Naturally I discussed it with George, who naturally thought it a good idea for me to take up the offer. After all, that way he'd have his supervisor at hand – for by then I had agreed to take him on – and he would undertake to find me accommodation.

And so, in steamy August 1984 I saw for the first time the flat on Acharnon Street. George was waiting at the airport and quickly ushered Pauline and me through the NOTHING TO DECLARE exit, himself carrying the audiovisual machine he'd asked me to buy for him in England – 'here they are too expensive' – and which I'd wrapped in newspaper and forced into a plaid shopping bag, the kind of bag I associated with bottles of stout and scrag-end of lamb. 'If you are stopped, say it is a teaching aid for your own use,' George had instructed me, but the bored customs officials showed no interest in any of our luggage. They didn't even query George's presence at my side. Why should they? As soon as passengers had shown themselves within the arrivals hall, those waiting for them had simply pushed past the would-be restraining arms of the airport police and now whole families were assisting in the task of carrying off those many boxes, parcels, cases and bags without which, it seems, no Greek can travel. We climbed into the back of George's scratched and badly dented Lada – 'two or three crashes, nothing to worry about' – and headed for the city.

Street after street of nondescript concrete-built apartment blocks stretched away into the surrounding hills, most of them with an unfinished or somehow provisional look about them: bare brick here, unglassed windows there, and everywhere steel rods sticking up from the flat rooftops. The road itself was littered with discarded newspapers, plastic bags, rusting coke tins; and floatings of cement dust drifted through what appeared to be rotting sunlight and was, so I would find out, caused by the worst atmospheric pollution in the Western world.

Then the car journey was over and a very few moments later Pauline, George and I were somehow crammed into a lift. 'By the way,' George said, as the lift groaned its way upward, 'never use this if the electricians are going to strike. You may be trapped for hours.'

'How will I know if they're going to strike?'

He shrugged. 'If I know, I will tell you.' The lift stopped and we hauled my luggage out onto a bare landing before following him through a door whose lock had been recently and none too professionally fitted.

'Well?' he asked.

A three-piece suite of worn red plush took up most of the floor space of the tiny lounge. There was also, I noticed, a glass-topped coffee table and a set of straight-backed chairs with rush seats, lined up against a wall papered with a motif that looked very like elephants' bums and facing a cheap wooden bookcase. But what really took my attention was the man who swayed uncertainly on top of a pair of stepladders that straddled the polished wood floor. 'This is father,' George said. 'He is called Manolis. He is fixing your light.'

Manolis began a careful descent of the ladders. He must have been all of eighteen stone, perhaps more, and his round face and near-bald head, to which wisps of grey hair clung damply, was pink and beaded with sweat. A pair of grey trousers had been let out at the sides to fit around his enormous belly and above them he wore a short-sleeved cotton vest. We shook hands – his hand was wet – and when he smiled his mouth opened to reveal pink, bare gums. (I would later discover that he only ever put his teeth in for important family occasions.) But the smile was one of great sweetness and it reached up to his blue-grey eyes. 'Welcome,' he said, uttering the word with grave deliberation, and after a moment added, 'Yannis.' He pointed to me. 'You Yannis,' he said, 'me Manolis.'

'And this is Pauline,' I said. Manolis shook hands with her and then once again shook hands with me.

He went over to the light switch, snapped it on and stared up at the bulb. The bulb, unlit, dangled from bare flex which was suspended from an elaborately carved ceiling rose, barely held in place by the one screw allotted it. Manolis tried the switch again. The bulb remained unlit. 'No good,' he said to us all and shrugged, an expansive world-weary heave of his shoulders. Then he gathered up his ladders and left.

The shrug intrigued me. 'It looked as though your father was thinking the Greek for "*dolce far niente*",' I suggested. But George shook his head.

'No,' he said, 'he was thinking the Greek for "oh fuck it".'

I went to the balcony and looked out. And it was then I began to understand why George had been anxious about his choice of flat. In the first place it stank. Acrid fumes of cheap petrol and diesel, the hot smells of abraded rubber and brake shoes slammed against wheel rims, all drifted up from the traffic-clogged road on which my apartment block stood. As they rose they mingled with fumes from the oil-fired boiler in the basement. This was supposed to fuel the air-conditioning system during the summer and, in winter, supply us with central heating. But the air conditioning never worked and as for the central heating, I would learn that on the few occasions it did operate it provided only two 'shots' a day, and by the time the water had struggled up to my fourth-floor flat it did little more than take the worst chill off the radiators. God knows how people on the seventh, top, floor managed. But if the warm water didn't rise, the boiler fumes most certainly did.

So did the stench from the butcher's shop next door. Each weekday morning, early, the butcher would start to boil bones. Maggoty sweet smells crawled in through the flat's open windows and clung to curtains, chairs, even my clothes. I thought of Mr Guppy and his friend and of their discovery of Krook's death by spontaneous combustion, of the smouldering, suffocating vapour and thick, nauseating pool of grease into which Guppy inadvertently dipped his fingers. On bad mornings I could imagine pools like that forming on the floor of my flat. After some months the smells lessened and finally died away, although I could never believe the flat was entirely free of them. The butcher had shut up shop, I don't know why. I do know that on that first afternoon of cloudy, oppressive heat, the smell from his shop seemed to be coming from some pit of final corruption.

Then there were the noises. I didn't find out about all of these until later. For example, the frantic sexual activity in the flat above me only began in the late autumn. The woman who had moved into the flat was English, perhaps in her mid-thirties, had staring blue eyes, wore a variety of two-piece costumes – powder blue and damson were among her favourite colours – doused herself in cheap scent, and on the few occasions I met her was either accompanying a different man into or out of the apartment block or opening my mail. She was able to do this because each morning the postman would leave the mail for the entire block on a small desk inside the foyer. You had to go down and retrieve what was yours. The first time I did so the woman from upstairs was standing by the desk reading a letter. 'It's for you,' she said accusingly. It was only when I'd climbed back upstairs to my flat that I allowed myself to wonder at her behaviour. Did she often open other people's letters? Had she gone off with any? And why did she do it? Did she perhaps think that letters from England, even when not addressed to her, might ease the loneliness that stared from her eyes? I don't suppose the men did. They never seemed to stay for more than an hour, although during that time there'd be noise aplenty: shrieks, shouts, doors slammed and, inevitably, what sounded like the thump of a pile driver and must have been the bed, tested to its limits.

Once, when we found ourselves alone in the lift, she told me her Greek husband was a ship's engineer, away for months at a time. 'I work as a hotel receptionist,' she said, as though that explained something. Her voice was light, expressionless, ironed-out Cockney. 'I'm teaching at the University,' I told her. 'Really?' She was already bored. 'I wouldn't call that man's work,' she said, 'not a real man anyway.' After that, I never dared ask whether she'd stashed any of my post.

Other noises invaded my flat: of family quarrels, of occasional parties, of a small boy induced into screaming fits by a screaming mother, of a howling dog in the flat next door. But none of these could ever compare with the noises that came up from the street. Most of the year the windows stayed open. Since the air conditioning didn't work, I had the choice of being slowly suffocated by fumes that leaked from the air ducts or of putting up with the street's uproar. I chose the latter.

Somewhere in the world there may be a noisier street than Acharnon Street; but I hope not. A six-lane highway leading straight into the city centre, it was as busy at three a.m. as at three o'clock in the afternoon. All night long queues of nose-to-tail cars, lorries, coaches, taxis and motorbikes filled Acharnon Street, howling to a sudden halt (there was a set of traffic lights almost outside my window), blurting horns when red turned to green (you could just about hear them above the revving, farting engines whose drivers, in their macho determination to be first away when the lights changed, kept their accelerators fully pressed down, those in the front row always inching beyond the lights with the result that they couldn't see when the change came and so relied on the cars behind them to signal the off); and then they'd career towards the next set of lights under a haze of exhaust fumes, tyres screeching on the road's marble surface as though the drills of a thousand dentists had been wired up for some megafest of electronic sound.

As the year wore on I became inured to the night noises. Noise by day was different and once drove me nearly to distraction. I was in the flat that morning, trying to write, and as usual I had thrown open all the windows. Then the noise began. On this occasion it came not from Acharnon Street but from a narrow cut-through lane that connected Acharnon with the street parallel to it. The cut-through was supposed to be closed to all traffic except those using it for official purposes, including the garbage disposal cart that came around twice a week in order to collect the black plastic bags in which people put their rubbish. The bags were piled up beside the entrance to each apartment block and invariably split open before they could be collected, disgorging their malodorous contents across the pavement. On this particular morning the cart driver and his mates parked below my side window and went off to a nearby *kafeneion* for coffee and no doubt ouzo. They'd been gone all of five minutes when two cars drove up behind the cart and couldn't get past. Of course they shouldn't have been there, but you wouldn't have guessed that from the persistent fury with which the drivers began to sound their horns. After ten minutes of this the driver of the cart and his mates returned, not, however, to move off, but to remonstrate with the car drivers for daring to use a lane forbidden to them. To make themselves heard above the blaring horns meant they had to shout very loudly indeed. Then the driver of the cart got up into his cab and began to sound *his* horn. At this, the car drivers got out of their cars and began to shout at him and his mates. More people arrived and began to shout at the car drivers, the driver of the cart, his mates, and at each other. This went on until the driver of the cart jumped down and shook hands with one of the car drivers, an act which proved to be the signal for a general hand shaking and slapping of backs; and then, when everyone's hand had been shaken by everyone else, the entire group headed for the *kafeneion*. As they disappeared through its doors a car drove up behind the two parked cars and the garbage disposal cart and was unable to pass them. There being no sign that the cars or cart were about to move, the driver began to sound his horn. At that point I decided to cut my losses and go downtown to the British Council library.

Anyone who has lived in Athens for no matter how short a period of time will be able to cap that story. What you get on Acharnon is what you get at any major Athenian square or intersection. Twenty-four-hour wall-to-wall *noise*. The implosive crump as cars drive into each other, the two-tone bray of police vans and the wail of an ambulance's siren; the street arguments as drivers leap from their vehicles to claim right of way, dispute who cut in on who, who deliberately parked in a certain place reserved for another, who did or did not indicate he wanted to turn right before turning left (or vice versa), whose mother had given birth to thirty devils, whose father was the Antichrist, whose sister deserved to marry a Turk, whose uncle had a sealed anus... The insults are as ritualised as the all-purpose swear word *malakas* and gestures: the spread five-finger thrust of dismissal, the two-handed chop at your own crotch ('my balls'), the backward jerk of the head ('a thousand times NO!'). Well, but if you could find all this anywhere in Athens, what was so special about Acharnon Street? Simple. Acharnon Street had brothels.

They'd arrived, so George later told me, during the period of the junta. In the early years of the century most brothels had been down at Piraeus, Athens' port town. Although it now feels like a suburb of the city, Piraeus possessed for many years its own 'wide-open' identity, and in the '20s and '30s the brothels of Pireaus were notable for their association with *rembetika* and hashish. According to Gail Holst, the music's historian, *rembetika*'s roots were in the jail-and-hashish songs of the criminal underworld of Asia Minor. Following the disaster of 1922, when over a million Greeks were forced out of Asia Minor, the music migrated to Greece from the Turkish mainland. Piraeus was an obvious home for it. It's almost gone now. I was told of *rembetika* cafés round Exarcha Square, not far from the university, but on the couple of occasions I went there I found students and student lookalikes being herded into police vans. 'It's a drugs bust,' I was told. Of the music itself there was no sound. *Rembetika* had become a code word for drug dealing.

There are still brothels in Piraeus but they're strictly for the sailors. Others, including tourists, are catered for elsewhere. The tourists started to arrive in growing numbers in the late '50s, Americans mostly, but with a scattering of students from north European countries. Their favourite Athenian haunt was the Plaka. With its handsome neoclassical buildings, winding, narrow, cobbled streets, and steep-step passages spreading out from directly below the Acropolis, the Plaka was, as it still is, the last of old Athens. Here you could find some of the city's best – as well as worst – tavernas, where intellectuals, musicians, writers and politicians came to eat, drink and argue. Here, too, was the famous fleamarket. And here, not surprisingly, brothels began to appear, a few at first and then more and still more until there were brothels in just about every quarter of the Plaka.

Then, in 1967, the American-backed junta of colonels assumed control of the nation. The Plaka was to be cleaned up. So the brothels had to go. Of course they didn't close. They simply moved on. Acharnon was as good a spot as any: easy to get to by taxi or on foot, plenty of apartments for rent, and in an unfashionable part of the city where Papadopoulos's police rarely bothered to venture. There must have been hundreds of brothels within a stone's throw of my flat, and promptly at nine o'clock each evening they'd switch on the single sodium-yellow light which hung above their street doors. The Greek sense of time is at best approximate. 'I'll meet you at noon' translates into 'let's try to make it by three o'clock'. But the brothels really did all open on time. You could have set your watch by them.

As soon as the yellow light came on the first punters would arrive. There was nothing furtive about them. They didn't behave as novels and black-and-white films of the 1950s had told me such men did.

This was a world away from whispers at lampposts, calls from doorways – 'Hallo, dearie, fancy a good time' – from the scuttle for privacy up evil-smelling back stairs.

Young men came first, among them some who couldn't have been more than fifteen or sixteen. They'd ride up on every kind of mechanised two-wheel transport, from scooters through to the most powerful motorbikes, usually in gangs of four or more, seldom anyone on his own. For several minutes they'd sit astride their machines, shouting to each other above their constantly revving engines, sometimes roar away, but more often than not dismount, lean their bikes against each other and troop through the door. Thirty minutes later they'd reappear, kick their engines back to life and ride off towards the city centre, the pig-squeal of their tyres soon lost in the street's wash of noise. '*Maridha*' George called them, small fry. But they must be allowed to visit prostitutes, he said, because that kept them from 'pure girls'. No self-respecting Greek man would marry a woman who was not a virgin.

Later at night it would be the turn of the big sharks: middle-aged men. They came by car or taxi. (Never close a door quietly when you can slam it, never pay a cab driver without shouting an exchange, and if you're the cab driver never drive off without first checking that your horn is in good working order.) George and I would pass groups of these men as we walked to Babi's taverna. I'd find myself wondering whether among them was the father of one of my students, a young woman who'd told me that when she was a little girl she and her mother had been locked into their flat each day by the father as he set off for work, and that he'd frequently not reappear before midnight. 'But what about shopping,' I asked, 'what of all the times your mother must have needed to go out?' Her father would accompany them, I was told. His wife wasn't to be trusted to go anywhere alone. When I told this to George he showed no surprise. 'Greek men are jealous for their women's honour,' he said. 'And he will have gone to a brothel in the evening, of that you can be sure. Paying good money for what he could get free at home. Me, I would rather spend money on food.'

'So would I,' I said. And at Babi's the food was always excellent. That was the best thing about the flat on Acharnon Street. It was only two minutes' walk from my favourite taverna.

Postcard from an Island

A six a.m. rooster's on morning call,
and here come hills shaping up for day.

When I put my foot through water, small fish
bicker round an inexplicable *kouros*.

Midday sun stirs deep, sweet scents,
though '*ochia* hide in fig trees', friends warn,

'they thirst after fig-milk', ash-grey branches
condominiums for small ash-grey snakes.

'It's a rime-riche world' I tell them, like those stacked
lion-mane terraces where goats browse, their bells'

tink, *tink* drying on valley air, or this pair
of bag-uddered cows who sashay past our hotel

at ouzo hour's pure floating of white –
doves above their towery, white-stone cotes.

Later, through thyme-spiked
owl-whickery dark

we'll reach the world's edge, hear
sea turn over in its moony sleep.

CHAPTER TWO

Discoveries

BY COINCIDENCE, a colleague and friend at Loughborough University, Gurth Higgin, was due to arrive in Athens on the same day as us, bringing with him his wife, daughter and a son. They were on their way to somewhere in the Peloponnese where they were to attend a wedding. 'Stay with us,' I'd grandly offered before we left England. So they did. But four became seven when the daughter extended the offer to a trio of women singers with whom she was friendly. The singers were, I think, called the Belle Stars, had made a record, treated themselves and us as though they were important people, and were strictly vegetarian. This led to a pronounced *froideur* when George took the entire party to a taverna which specialised in roast goat. The next morning the seven of them left early.

Later that day I phoned the university, hoping to speak to Professor R. 'Please to contact me as soon as you are in Athens,' he had written in response to a letter of mine in which I'd told him the date of our arrival. 'I will be at my desk awaiting you.' But he wasn't. No matter. For the next few days we pounded the streets, visiting the National Gallery and the Museum of Byzantine Art, at both of which we found many rooms closed to the public (this, I would discover, was typical) and, altogether more fruitfully, the National Archaeological Museum. Nineteen eighty four happened to be the year when the row over *Black Athena* was at its height. A New York academic claimed that historians of classical Greece had formed a conspiracy of silence about the influence of North Africa on Greek art of the classical period. On our first visit to the museum we came upon a room given over to the massive *koroi*: larger than life-size figures of male youths carved out of sandstone, their near shoulder-length hair and facial features undoubtedly suggesting strong affinities with Egyptian art, the very stiffness of their pose and the slight advance of one foot indicating their possible origin in the frieze paintings of Egyptian tombs. These *koroi* were dated to the sixth and fifth century BC. Black Athena, then.

But then, turning a corner, we found ourselves confronted by figures sculpted no more than a hundred years later, in which the representation of the human body had, as though in the blinking of an eye, attained perfection. In musculature, proportion, sense of movement, of balance, of sheer beauty, these figures are the apogee of the human form divine. Later I would see their equivalent elsewhere – at Delphi and Olympia, for instance. But on that broiling hot August afternoon, gazing at the Neptune which had been drawn up in fishermen's nets as recently as 1928, I knew that the argument about Black Athena was entirely beside the point. For quite apart from Neptune, there was the wondrous sculpting of a young man sometimes identified as Perseus, and in addition the fragmentary boy on the horse; and between them these three works testified to a unique moment, the discovery of how to render the human body in a manner so complete that it has never been bettered. And though the great masters of the Italian Renaissance – Donatello, Michaelangelo, Bernini – would add a new emotional intensity (and sexiness) to their three-dimensional representations of the human figure, Neptune was beyond improvement: the musculature of his arms upraised in the act of hurling his trident, taut legs taking the strain of his body's poised weight in which you could even see the veins working, the perfectly proportioned head with its jutting beard.

As I studied the figure on its plinth a gaggle of young Japanese tourists came to stand around it. The women pointed to Neptune's buttocks before indicating, laughing as they did so, that they regarded their boyfriends' as altogether inferior. One young woman even made her partner pose beside Neptune, then snapped them both from the rear. In other circumstances I might have felt irritated by such seeming irreverence, but on this occasion it seemed an appropriate gesture of homage.

The next day I spent a long, boozy lunch with a member of the British Council at which several bottles of Cava Cambas were emptied and I mentioned that I was finding it impossible to contact Professor R. 'He's in America,' I was told, 'won't be back for another fortnight.'

'He gave me to understand he'd be here, in Athens.'

'Don't believe all you're told. Greece doesn't work like that. Might as well head off to an island. No point in hanging around Athens in this heat. The *nefos* is bloody awful, too. No breeze to shift it.'

Literally *nefos* means mist, and is the word by which Athenians refer to the dire pollution of their city. Even at the best of times a brown haze hangs over Athens, a thick blend of fumes from petrol, oil-fired central heating and air-conditioning, and factory chimneys, dimming the sun, clogging the nostrils and layering the tongue. And this wasn't the best of times. Without wind to disperse the poisonous mist, the *nefos was* bloody awful.

'Where do you suggest?'

'Try Sifnos,' he said, 'I'm told it's a green island.'

So the next morning Pauline and I took the metro down to Piraeus and bought tickets for a ferry leaving at four p.m. And that afternoon, for the first time, we sailed out into the Aegean.

Our boat, an old, creaking bucket of a ship, was crowded with backpackers, besides others like ourselves travelling more modestly; and then there were Greeks going home or visiting relatives on various of the islands – Tinos, Syros, Paros, Naxos – at which we stopped. Each time we came into port a scene of pure pandemonium would repeat itself. Those waiting to disembark would be herded together behind a rope stretched across the ship's bow, over which a seaman stood guard, watching the great steel plate lower to allow the exit and then entry of vehicles and foot passengers. Those waiting to embark would be similarly herded together behind a port policeman, gorgeous in shark-white uniform with epaulettes and gold braid, whistle clenched between his teeth. And all, whether on shore or on ship, would play a game of granny's footsteps. As soon as an official back was turned the crowd would hasten forward and, as it span round, the crowd would come to a crazed, teetering halt. There were men in black suits with stuffed suitcases under each arm and further cases dangling from their fingers, grey-shawled women with live fowls pressed to their bosoms, others with goods wrapped up in blankets and tablecloths, still others wailing tragically as they stood to greet or say farewell to friends and relatives they hadn't seen or wouldn't expect to see for (say) forty-eight hours; there were men whose occupation was to secure the ship's ropes to bollards – they were conscious of the cachet attached to their work and performed it with some style, a cigarette nonchalant at their lips; there were men who shouted at cars and trucks manoeuvring on or off the boat and who themselves were shouted at by the police, either because they were usurping the official's role or not doing their work to his satisfaction; there were men who rushed on board to sell bread sticks, soft drinks and camera film; and at the back of each quay were children holding aloft squares of cardboard advertising ROOMS TO RENT, NICE PLACES and, once, LOGGINGS HERE. Despite the seeming chaos, the ship seldom took longer than ten minutes to complete its turn-around and then we were once again sailing out into the Aegean.

As the journey went on, more and more people dropped ashore and there was now room to sit down. Pauline and I found some empty seats on deck from which, rapt in silence, we stared at the new world about us. How many blues is blue? There was blue sea to either side below us, there was flawless blue sky above, and in between sea and sky was blue air. Occasionally, the air would intensify as though gathering itself together, and we would stare hard at the spot, thinking that it might somehow indicate the shape of an island we were not scheduled to call at. And so, for all we knew to the contrary, it did, and it was easy to imagine that somewhere on the far side of that intense blue, on top of a hill we couldn't make out, a one-eyed giant sat listening to the steady throb of our ship's engines as we passed.

When we finally arrived at Sifnos, night had long since fallen, stars glittered above us, the sea had become an all-but-invisible susurrus with occasional streaks of curdling white. Then, out of the darkness, the lights of the port town of Kamares loomed up, and in a matter of minutes we were off the boat and standing on the quayside.

After we'd found lodgings near the harbour, we sat down to eat at a waterside taverna. As we lingered over salad and a grilled fish so sweetly clean you felt it must have been in the water not half an hour since, we watched a man drop from a rowing boat into thigh-deep water. Then he began to wade across to a taverna beyond ours. Hanging from his fingers was a fish some two feet long, its tail flicking slowly to and fro.

Next day we caught a bus to the middle of the small island and from there walked across to the so-called town of Kastri, past terraced fields sloping away to sea and, at one point, under a large fig tree, a chapel from which, as we passed, an old woman dressed all in black with black headscarf emerged to beckon us in. She wanted to show us a small well at the back of the chapel. We looked, nodded our approval of the bitter cold water she drew from it for us to taste, and when she held out her hand I dropped some coins into her palm. Only then were we allowed on our way.

From a distance, Kastri seemed no more than a handful of houses abutting a hillside above the sea, each house gleaming white and with vivid blue doors and window frames. Yet the streets were so mazily planned that we spent some time wandering about them without coming across any one street twice. No wonder the labyrinth is a Greek invention. All Greek island towns are similarly labyrinthine. Necessarily so. The confusion of streets was intended to bewilder and frustrate successive boatloads of pirates who over the centuries came to plunder, rape and kill. All that beauty, and what did men want? To destroy.

From the town we climbed down to a tiny horseshoe bay where I swam in waters so clear I could see fish thirty or so feet below me flicker in and out of black rock, and afterwards, looking out at flawless blue, we ate a late lunch of salad and cheese pies at a beach taverna we more or less had to ourselves.

Later, sitting over beers as we waited for a bus to take us back to Kamares, shaded by a huge plane tree under whose branches we could look out at green, terraced fields and, beyond, royal blue sea, the simmer of bees all around, breathing in the deep, sweet and, as it somehow seemed, tawny smells, I suddenly found myself remembering some lines of Donald Davie's, about fenland England.

> Yet a beauty there is, noble, defenceless, unshrinking,
> In being at somebody's mercy, wide and alone.

Why on earth had those lines come to me? Perhaps because the beauty of Sifnos – and it *was* beautiful, breathtakingly so – must often have left it at the mercy of, among others, Corsairs, Turks, Germans. Who did Davie have in mind when he wrote of the fens' defencelessness? The Vikings, perhaps. A brutally callous lot, certainly. But that had been a long time ago. Would Davie have written so calmly of being defenceless if those on whose unimaginable mercy dwellers in the fens depended had within living memory fallen on them, as had happened to the Sifniots? Alert to what he rightly sensed was a turning point in history, Henry James had at the beginning of the First World War mourned the passing in England of what he called the record of 'the long, safe centuries'. In the event, neither then nor in 1940 was England invaded. The idea, the beauty, the allure even of defencelessness comes easier if you have never experienced what it actually means to have the enemy swarm ashore and take your land from you.

And yet Sifnos was a peaceable island. Though one or two disco bars had established themselves on the far side of the harbour from where we lodged and ate at one or another of the waterfront tavernas, the sounds that floated across the night-time water were muted, as though the bars were embarrassed about their presence in this green place. And as they did not bother people, so few people bothered with them. Even the youngest of the visiting tourists seemed content to sit for long hours at the tavernas, eating, drinking, talking. As for the islanders, come evening the women dragged cane-bottomed chairs out of their houses, or sat on steps to knit and talk. The men grouped themselves at a harbour-side *ouzerie*, smoking, concentrating over

tavli boards, or threading strings of rosary beads – *koumboli* – through their fingers as they directed remarks at one another. It was animated, but what you heard all around was the sound of human voices, sometimes augmented by a wash of water as a fishing boat puttered into harbour and tied up, but all of it equable, at ease.

By eking out what little money we'd brought with us, we were able to stay four days. Late on our final night, restless from the warmth of our bedroom and unable to sleep, I went out and sat on the steps that climbed up to a lane behind the house where we had our 'rent-room'. The steps acted as a kind of open-air gallery to display items of pottery that came from the shop opposite. (Sifnos, we had learnt, was famous for its ceramics.) Within moments, the shop owner, an old man, had come to sit beside me. He could speak no English and beyond the merest handful of words I could speak no Greek, but it was plain that the requirements of hospitality drew him to sit in silent companionship with me. And so, for half an hour, during which he smoked two cigarettes and once nudged me to point to a constellation of stars to which I could put no name, we sat there, and, when at length I got up and raised a hand to signify farewell, he insisted on accompanying me to my door. I held out my hand and he took it, looked into my eyes, shook my hand and then put an arm round my shoulder as though considering whether to embrace me.

'Goodnight,' I said.

He bowed his head briefly, dropped his arm, smiled warmly and turned back to his shop. That act of simple courtesy was the moment I fell in love with Greece.

Back in Athens we found a message George had slipped under our door. 'Come to Sunday lunch', it said. 'I will call for you at one o'clock.' Lunch. George used the English word, but as we realised soon after we'd been installed in the apartment he shared with his mother and father, what we were in for had precious little in common with the light, informal meal I had expected. This was an altogether more serious affair. Not that George's parents dressed up for the occasion. His mother, short, her face semi-permanently darkened by a worried frown that all too rarely smoothed into laughter, had certainly made an effort to arrange her hair, and wore a plum-red dress, set off by a round gold brooch; but Manolis was in vest and old grey trousers spattered by evidence of his cooking duties. Other days Irinia cooked, but Sundays Manolis ran the kitchen. We sat on their wide balcony under an awning that kept the full heat of an August sun from our dazzled eyes, before us a table on which were arranged plates of sardines, strips of capsicum, long, pale green and, as I found out, hot peppers, cheese, both white and yellow, a large bowl of salad, glasses, a bottle of ouzo, a bowl of ice cubes, and plastic bottles filled with retsina. Manolis remained inside, clattering dishes and utensils, and from time to time shouting words among which *malakas* occurred with some frequency.

George poured ouzo for us all. 'First we drink this,' he said, 'then we will drink wine.' He forked up some sardines and gestured for us to help ourselves to whatever we fancied. I nibbled a slice of cheese, Pauline took some salad. George's mother handed round bread. I noticed that places were set for more than the five of us.

'Are you expecting other guests?' I asked.

George shrugged, 'Perhaps. Who knows? Father asks friends but they may not come.'

But during the course of what turned out to be a marathon meal, friends did indeed arrive to eat with George and his family. By the time Manolis appeared with a large plate of roughly-sliced beef and roast potatoes, we had been joined by an old man who was introduced as an uncle, a former seaman, thin as a fish-bone, and without a tooth in his head. He smoked incessantly, picked at a little food, but was more interested in talk. He told me he had sailed the world. 'Of all the ladies I saw, I prefer the Argentine ladies. I do not like the French ladies.'

'And the English?'

He raised his eyebrows and his mouth framed an elaborate *moue* of rejection. 'Cold. Like the weather.'

'Its cloudy climate and its chilly women,' I quoted.

'Who said that?'

'Byron.'

'A great man,' he said fervently. 'He helped Greece.' He tapped his chest. 'Greeks love Byron.'

Soon after that he left, pausing on the way out to exchange words with a newcomer, another man, though this one was altogether younger, more George's age, clean-shaven, eyes gleaming with mischief behind his spectacles. He greeted Manolis and Irinia, who were clearly delighted to see him, with elaborate, unselfconscious warmth, and then looked at us, the look one of eager enquiry, of friendliness in waiting. 'This,' George said, 'is Dimitris.'

A cousin, I wondered?

'We were at school together,' George said. 'He is my friend. He runs the laundry in the next street. All that you need to have cleaned, you must take to him.'

We shook hands and I had the impression of a man of great physical strength, also of considerable physical grace, all of whose movements were without fuss and yet fluent; if movements can be charming, then charming they were. What I didn't yet know was that Dimitris was a natural lord of misrule, a wildly comic character who could zoom from hilarity to black melancholy in the time it takes to say *mavros*, and who, for all his unreliability, was someone whose company I came to delight in. And this, despite the fact that there'd be times I would curse his failure to launder sheets or shirts I'd left with him, when he'd be sleeping off a hangover or when the shop would be locked up because he had temporarily left Athens to escape creditors and other less savoury types – George hinted at Dimitris's connections with the city's criminal underworld. And once or twice he borrowed money which he then couldn't repay.

But this was to come. For the moment all I saw was a man full of jokes, who could set the table aroar, who ate and drank with evident relish and yet whose gestures and way of handling his knife and fork were of great delicacy – I never saw anyone so expertly fillet fish as Dimitris (he would then crunch his way through all the bones) – and who always saw to it that everyone's plate was full and glass brimming. That afternoon he was solicitous, considerate, full of natural good manners. If he happened upon an especially tender piece of meat he would insist on sharing it with others. He complimented Manolis on his cooking, Irinia on her dress, and, in his imperfect yet dauntless English, he told Pauline and me of a recent experience of night-fishing with a friend when 'we lose our engine, we lose our oar, we going to drown but God save us by a wind that blow us to shore. You see, God he love sinners.' And then, his eyes bright with laughter, 'and the bigger the sinner, the bigger the wind.'

Other friends and relatives drifted in and out during the afternoon. When Dimitris finally stood up to leave, we went with him so that he could show us the location of his shop. On the corner of George's street, an old woman, shabbily dressed in black, sat on an upturned wooden crate and wiped a piece of bread across a dinner plate that she balanced on her knees.

'Why on earth was she eating out there?' I asked, as Dimitris led the way up the next street.

'She is poor,' he said. 'She not eat if people don't give her food. So people take it in turn to feed her.'

His words reminded me that, not long after we'd arrived in Athens, Pauline and I had sat at a café in the Plaka, and had watched a queue of old women at a kebab stall opposite. The stall was doing a steady trade with tourists, but every so often, as the women waited patiently in line, the man operating the kebab would smuggle each in turn one of the pitta breads he'd surreptitiously filled with meat. No money changed hands, nor did he so much as look at the women. But as soon as they had received their filled pittas, the women shuffled away with food that for all we knew to the contrary was the only meal they could expect to have that day.

Later that week I tried yet again to contact Professor R. Again I had no luck. Ought I perhaps to go up to the building where the English department was housed? According to George the department was having to make do with temporary accommodation – an old hotel – while the building of a new university campus slowly neared completion.

'Why bother?' George said. 'Nobody will be there and there is nothing to see. Go to another island.'

It seemed good advice, especially as our daughter Emma, fresh from her first year as a university student, was due to join us. But which island could compare with the beauty of Sifnos?

'Try Spetses,' my contact at the British Council suggested. 'It's another green island, and no cars or motorbikes are allowed, so it's peaceful too.'

And so, a couple of days after we'd collected Emma from Athens airport, we went down to Piraeus and booked tickets for the afternoon ferry to Spetses, the island at the farthest reach of the Saronic gulf.

First port of call was Aegina. The ferry docked, unloaded, loaded, and then, moments later, reversed engines and prepared to sail on. Much hallooing from the quayside. The captain had forgotten to take on some essential cargo. Back into port went the ferry, this time at speed. There was a mighty thwack as the front of the boat hit the dock, and a tremor ran through the entire ship. Then, nothing. After several minutes, during which the boat gave no sign of further movement, passengers began to look at one another. Someone called down to a member of the crew who was standing in the half-open bow, presumably wanting to know what had happened. The sailor shrugged.

A short time later we became aware that the entire ship's crew had clambered off the ferry and were now to be seen walking towards the waterfront away from the vessel. There seemed nothing for it but to join them. As we dropped ashore, a small, dapper man with a thin moustache, who had been sitting near us on deck with his wife, approached me. 'I am a Syrian lawyer,' he said. 'You will come with me and we will sort this matter out.'

Quite why I had been picked out as his assistant I had no idea, but as he seemed to have a plan of action, I went with him. The lawyer marched towards a man who was leaning against a bicycle. 'This is the representative of the shipping line,' the lawyer said, as we drew close, 'we will accost him.' Arriving in front of the representative, whom he seemed to know, he began to harangue him in Greek. Judging from the way he counted off on his fingers, he was making a number of demands of the representative. When he stopped speaking, the representative spoke for some moments before mounting his bicycle and riding off in the direction of the waterfront.

'I perceive we are among crooks,' the lawyer said. Apparently the man had refused to accept any responsibility for the accident. Not only that, he had told the lawyer that there would be no compensation for our interrupted boat trip, that the next ferry would not be until morning, and that we would have to find our own accommodation for the night.

'The next ferry will depart at quarter-past-nine tomorrow morning,' the lawyer said. 'It is disgraceful.' I was inclined to agree, though whether his remark was aimed at the representative's denial of responsibility or the lack of an overnight ferry I couldn't tell.

'Will our tickets be valid?' I asked.

'I have been told so. But I take nothing on trust, and neither should you, my friend. If necessary, we must be prepared to fight our way on board. All of us.' The last words were directed to the rapidly dwindling band of disembarked passengers who stood about, variously disconsolate, puzzled, or resigned. The rest, an altogether larger number, had presumably already gone in search of rooms. Perhaps they were used to mishaps.

Pauline pointed to where, more or less opposite, a sign said PORT POLICE. 'We may as well try there,' she said.

I went across the road and found some stairs leading up to a half-open door on which was pinned a hand-written notice that said 'French and English speaking here'. In the room beyond, a heavily overweight man in dark-blue serge uniform, feet up on the desk, slept in his tilted-back chair. I knocked, coughed, shuffled my feet, and after a few minutes he opened his eyes and incuriously looked me up and down. In French I asked him whether he spoke French. By way of reply he got up and left the room. I waited. He did not return. After about fifteen minutes, I too left.

An hour later we managed to find rooms at a small hotel behind the church at the end of Aegina's waterfront. Relieved, we went for a swim at the town beach, then ate at a nearby taverna, spent some time wandering the back streets of the small port town and then, early next morning, went down to the port, determined not to miss our ferry. Emma pointed out that the ferry which had brought us to the island and which had apparently been disabled had in fact disappeared.

'Perhaps it sank,' Pauline said.

Eventually, at about ten a.m., a half-full boat bound for Spetses rounded the point to our right and in company with many of the previous day's passengers, including the Syrian lawyer (who I now realised bore a close resemblance to King Hussein of Jordan) and his wife, we went on board. Sailing away from Aegina, it never occurred to me that the island where we had reluctantly spent a night would come to mean so much to me, would be the Greek place that I would learn to love above all others. I wanted to get to Spetses, that green island where John Fowles had lived and taught, and where he had written *The Magus*.

And, after calls at Methena (an isthmus of the mainland) and the islands of Poros and Hydra, and having stood at the stern to watch dolphins playing in the wake of our boat as we steered away from the latter island, we arrived at Spetses shortly after midday. We were among the last to disembark. On the quay the Syrian lawyer stood arguing with one of the crewmen. That is to say, he argued, the crewman shrugged. All the lawyer's luggage had apparently been by mistake offloaded at Methena. Guiltily, we stole away in search of accommodation.

And then disaster, or what at the time felt like disaster. We found rooms, went for a swim, Pauline slipped on some rocks, fell, broke her wrist. The nurse at the port town's medical centre could do no more for her than put her arm in a sling and give her some painkillers. By early evening the three of us were back in the stifling heat of our flat on Acharnon Street. Once there, I phoned some English people in Athens – friends of friends – who, soon after our arrival, had contacted us to say that we should call on them 'any time' we needed help. They couldn't help. They had a social evening planned. Oh, thanks.

I phoned George, and within minutes George, dear, kind George, had arrived. He was due at a party but first he would take us to a hospital where Pauline could have her wrist x-rayed and, presumably, set and put in plaster.

Leaving Emma in the flat, we set off in George's car, Pauline by now in considerable pain. On the way George stopped to deliver some wine to the apartment where the party was being held, and while he was out of the car I went up to a nearby roadside kiosk hoping to buy some painkillers. Not surprisingly, the woman crouched inside the kiosk did not understand my request. I pointed to Pauline, clearly visible in the rear seat of the Lada, her arm in a sling. Ah, yes, now she understood. She smiled, nodded, and, after a moment's scrabbling on a lower shelf, handed out a packet of condoms.

In the corridor of the hospital's accident and emergency unit we came upon two men leaning against a wall, dressed in blood-stained coats that must once have been white, both of them smoking. They looked as though they had come straight from an abattoir and turned out to be doctors. But they set Pauline's wrist efficiently – though without anaesthetic so that she screamed when they forced the broken bones into place – and then, at the end of a long, long day, George was able to take us back to our apartment, and while Pauline went to get what rest she could, Emma and I ran over all that had happened since we had left Acharnon Street the previous morning. Shipwreck, lost property, broken bones. 'The curse of Spetses' we called it.

A few days later, our son Ben arrived with a girlfriend who, like him, was a student at Liverpool University. The two of them went off with Emma, island-hopping; and then it was time for Pauline, arm in sling, to leave. George – who else? – drove us to the airport. I was reluctant to let her go, but her sense of duty ruled out any possibility of her using a broken wrist as an excuse for deferring or cancelling the teaching she was due to start almost as soon as she stepped off the plane. 'He did his duty,' Jarndyce says of Neckett in *Bleak House*, and with his feckless friend Harold Skimpole in mind adds, 'he might have done worse. He might have undertaken to do it, and then not done it.'

So Pauline went back to Nottingham and I went back to Acharnon Street. Ben, Victoria and Emma returned from their island visits, and soon they, too, left for England. It was now getting towards the end of September, I had not been paid by the university – I realised that I didn't even know *how* I was to be paid – and still there was no communication from Professor R. I had phoned, I had written, I had by now dropped in on the department and left a letter in his pigeon-hole. Nothing. I filled my days by beginning work on a study of modern English poetry I had promised to deliver to Batsford by the end of 1985, by occasionally visiting Dimitris's laundry to deliver or collect clothes and sheets – I would be motioned to the chair which, as in all Greek shops, was strategically placed for the convenience of customers who wanted to talk (talk was taken for granted: you couldn't simply do business); and of an evening I tried out various local tavernas or, more rarely, considered spending the evening alone, though by mid-evening the heat and street noises would customarily force me out into the warm night air, to saunter along the thronged pavements, perhaps stopping for a drink at a bar or to order a coffee and cognac at a wayside *zakaraplasteion*, where you could buy *glyktisma* – cakes rich in nuts or dripping with honey – and where I found the Greek brandy, poured with careless generosity, much to my liking, its vanilla flavour giving it a riper, deeper bouquet than its French counterpart, which by comparison now seemed thin, even acidulous.

Then, one Friday evening, George suggested I should accompany him to a taverna on the far side of Athens, where he wanted to introduce me to two friends of his who were, he explained, anxious to meet me. 'They are called Manos and Fotini. You will like them.'

Manos and Fotini were waiting for us when we arrived – of all the Greeks I know they are the only ones who make a habit of being on time – and my first impression was of a couple whose elegance of dress and manners were in such sharp contrast to George's casual ways as to make their friendship unlikely to the point of downright improbable. Yet the three were plainly fond of each other. Over Italian food – they had chosen a pizzeria for our first meeting – Manos, who wore a well-cut sports coat and sported a trim beard, told me that he and George had known each other for many years, and that they were now colleagues, teaching English to more or less reluctant officer recruits at the Military Academy. As for Fotini, beautiful, with large, lustrous eyes, a perfectly-proportioned oval face, and dressed in impeccable denim jacket and trousers, she was, she explained, a translator who also acted as a guide to various tourist companies and, in addition, gave private language lessons.

Like all Greeks, Manos and Fotini worked hard, harder than seemed feasible, let alone sensible. From eight a.m. until one p.m. Manos taught at the Academy, then in the afternoon he had several private classes, and in the evening taught again, this time at a language school – a *frontistirion* – owned by his boss at the Academy but fronted by the boss's wife, because government-paid officials were not supposed to moonlight. Of course, everyone did. As I already knew, George ran his own small language school, and in the months to follow I would discover that my students also worked in language schools or gave 'privates'. What they learnt by day, they taught by night.

> So naturalists observe a flea,
> Hath smaller fleas that on it prey;
> And these have smaller fleas to bite'em,
> And so proceed, ad infinitum.

As for Fotini, when not translating novels and philosophic treatises into Greek from French, German and English for a publisher who paid her far too little, she was sitting on a coach speaking any or all of those languages plus Spanish, Italian and Russian to tourists, and as an added bonus dealing with disgruntled passengers who claimed their tour company had misled them and that they wanted their money back – 'We were promised that the Acropolis was on top of Olympus,' one had allegedly insisted; and when she wasn't following either of these vocations she was to be found working part-time in a language school, oh, and giving her 'privates', of course. Mustn't forget those. Merely to hear their work schedules made me feel faint.

As we chatted on that first evening, I learnt that neither had a degree from the University of Athens. Instead, they were graduates of the London External degree course. And both had been taught by Robert Liddell.

'Do you know him?' Manos asked.

'I know who he is. One of the writers who came to Greece before the war, a friend of Durrell, and, for all I know, of Reggie Smith, Bernard Spencer... those ex-pats who feature in Olivia Manning's *Balkan Trilogy*. I met Bernard Spencer, once, in a pub in Soho,' I told them. 'He was a friend of my great friend, Ian Fletcher. They'd all been in Cairo during the war. Ian and George Fraser, others.'

Manos wasn't sure he had heard of Ian, but he knew of the rest. He had, I gathered, made regular use of Fraser's *The Modern Writer and his World*, and was intrigued to learn that after George's death, in 1980, Ian and I had edited his poems. (Though not his translations, the publishers hadn't wanted those, fine though they were.)

'He wrote some poems about the Middle East, I think?'

'He did indeed,' I told him, 'as did Ian. Did you know that Ian has been collecting an archive of poems written by wartime servicemen who fought in the desert?'

The longer we talked, the more it became apparent that Manos, who now told me he had been born in Alexandria, the city of Cavafy, whose poetry he loved, was extraordinarily well read in the literatures of Europe and of America. But he had an especial interest in all those British writers, whether fighting men or civilians, who had been in the Middle East – Cairo, Alexandria – during the Second

World War. I couldn't share his enthusiasm for Durrell's *Alexandrian Quartet* but we were able to agree on the excellence of Olivia Manning's *Balkan* and *Levant* trilogies.

Towards the end of a convivial evening Manos suddenly asked, 'Do you think it would be possible to produce a thesis on such writers?'

Ah, so that was what lay behind the invitation to eat with them. Not that I minded. 'I don't see why not,' I said.

'I told him you would agree,' George said, beaming at us all.

It wasn't what I had said, but never mind. And anyway, by the time we parted I had agreed to take Manos on as a doctoral student. I'd also gladly accepted his offer to introduce me to Robert Liddell.

'Be careful, John,' Fotini said, who was evidently no great admirer of Liddell. 'He farts, you know. Uncontrollably,' she added.

The meeting took place one lunchtime a week later at the British Council offices in Kolonaki Square. Manos was waiting for me in the foyer, impeccably dressed as at our previous meeting, and with a copy of that week's *Times Literary Supplement* tucked under his arm. He had, I now noticed, a slight stoop, more perhaps a droop of his shoulders, as though inured to the world and its ways, but alert to its absurdities and prepared to suffer them. 'Manos, the world-weary Alexandrian,' I took to calling him, a soubriquet that he acknowledged with a wry smile.

In the intervening week I had managed to read Liddell's excellent biography of Cavafy, to look through his *Treatise on the Novel*, which seemed an engaging if unoriginal exercise along the lines of Forster's *Aspects of the Novel*, and had failed to make headway with a novel whose hero was an ex-public school, Oxford-educated lecturer working in the Middle East and surrounded by comic foreigners and uncouth ex-pats. All of these books I'd taken out of the British Council Library, which was especially rich in holdings by British writers who had spent time in Greece. Many of these books were in fact inscribed copies, made out to the Council Library. (A year or two later, I should note, the library was virtually dismantled at the whim of a Thatcher-inspired diktat: books were out, computers were in. Manos took it upon himself to wheel a shopping trolley down to Kolonaki Square and for a pittance bought literally hundreds of books the Council was forced to get rid of: I'm pleased he was able to give the books a good home but remain appalled at the cultural vandalism that led to the break-up of so invaluable a collection.)

Liddell was waiting for us in the small coffee lounge on the first floor. Old, frail, and ill-looking, he was dressed in a blue shirt and baggy, creased grey trousers. Thin, grey-white hair lay in strands across a curiously flat crown, and his eyes, bloodshot and red-rimmed, peered at us from behind thick glasses. He greeted Manos, of whom he was clearly fond, warmly, called him 'Mano,' and gave me his hand to shake. I don't recall a great deal of our conversation, which was mostly literary small talk. Yes, he had met G S Fraser, and had been present on an occasion when Olivia Manning had snapped at him. Apparently Reggie Smith, her philandering husband, had brought Fraser and others, including Liddell, back to the Mannings' apartment in war-time Cairo after an evening's boozing. She was tired and plainly angered by her husband's convivial plans, and as a way of hinting that the others should take themselves off, announced that she was going to bed. 'Ah,' George said, in a clumsy attempt to placate and perhaps charm her. ' "She walks in beauty like the night". Keats,' he added by way of explanation.

'Byron, you fool,' she said.

Liddell also told me that Lawrence Durrell had once remarked to him that 'everyone congratulates me on the success of the *Quartet*. Nobody congratulates me on its merit.' And he spoke interestingly about the Greek reluctance to pursue literary criticism 'as we understand it. Even Seferis, God rest his noble soul, is inclined to rhapsodise.' I later found he had written virtually the same words in an essay on Seferis. I asked him if he was working on anything new. No, but he was busy revising his Cavafy biography for another edition, and had just finished correcting the proofs of his book on Iris Murdoch and Ivy Compton Burnett.

'Do you approve of their work?' he asked. Sensing that discretion was the better part of candour, I said that to my shame I wasn't really familiar with either, but that I greatly admired Henry Green's fiction. He nodded, though whether in agreement or because my remark had confirmed his judgement of my tastes I've no idea. He mentioned that he had seen one or two of my poetry reviews in *The New Statesman* 'but I am so out of touch that the names of the poets you mention mean nothing to me. I must say, though, that all this talk of Martianism seems dreadfully silly. To see the world as a strange place is surely what *any* good writer does?'

As we rose to take our leave, he put his hand on Manos's arm. 'I am delighted you are taking your studies further,' he said. 'And I look forward to what you have to say about us all. I will, of course, be pleased to answer any questions you may have. Remember, dear Mano, those were difficult times.' I had the feeling that he was anxious as to what Manos might say about him.

Afterwards, at a café where we stopped for a sandwich and glass of wine, Manos asked me what I had made of Liddell. 'Well,' I said, 'he wasn't about to reveal too much of himself, was he? Understandable, perhaps. He probably thinks of me as one of the barbarians in waiting. He belongs to a world that scarcely exists any longer, in England at all events.'

'I think he yearns for such an England,' Manos said. 'You know, once, when I was reading from *Sense and Sensibility*, he stopped me when I pronounced Colonel Brandon's waistcoat wrongly, or wrongly as he thought. "Dear Mano," he said, "a gentleman always says weskit."'

'I suppose there's a dwindling band of literary ex-pats like Liddell for whom David Cecil is *le dernier cri* of critical opinion.'

'And Lord Dunsany?'

'He was an old idiot, wasn't he? The character based on him gets bumped off in the *Balkan Trilogy*. A good way of ridding the world of that kind of snobbish *belle-lettrist* nonsense.' And I quoted John Wain's characterising of Cecil's style as 'a mixture of pointless inversions, half-hearted exclamations, and a general air of twittering.' I also told him that John had on more than one occasion left me helpless with laughter at his impression of Cecil's lecturing manner, its bird-like swoops and glissades, the flutter of fingers, the manner in which he would suddenly gape wordlessly at his audience as though, John said, he had become aware of some dangerous insect crawling up the inside of his trouser leg.

'I don't think Robert approved of Dunsany,' Manos said.

'Well,' I said, 'good for him.'

Among the Barbarians

The boys are still hopeful:
dark eyes gleaming
they offer *jig-a-jig*.

Ah, hotel afternoons
Cavafy's poems led him to.
The shuttered windows, those
   learned lusts.

Now he's too old for that
busy with other work in hand.
Jane Austen's Vanished World

which few, he fears, will read,
and yet such grace
and *such* discretion…

In Kolonaki Square he sips
frappé, seeing it all:
tea-cups white on the lawn

as Darcy's head is turned
by Knightley's perfect wit
and Marianne will read to him

Cowper until the coachman
   comes:
'a temper rustic
as the life we lead'.

He sighs and stirs
in the quick chill
of this car-maddened space.

What is he doing here?
Settling his empty glass
he studies suds of froth

that cling like… like
malakas he thinks unstoppably,
and Captain Wentworth smiles.

CHAPTER THREE

The University

BY LATE SEPTEMBER my days had fallen into a routine. An early breakfast of coffee and oranges, though no complacencies of the peignoir. Most mornings I was at my typewriter by eight o'clock or making my way downtown to work in the British Council library. At different times each day I would phone the university with predictable lack of success. No, Professor R was not in. No, his whereabouts were not known. No, only he would be able to tell me how and when I would be paid.

Then, one morning at the end of the month, the phone rang and, glory be, I found myself speaking to Professor R. Why, he wanted to know, had I made no attempt to contact him? For some time he had been expecting me to introduce myself and now, having been at pains to discover my telephone number, he was required to contact *me*. He sounded decidedly put out, as though I had not only transgressed against obvious courtesies but had imposed a Sisyphean labour on a very busy man.

'I've been trying to contact you for the past month,' I said.

'I am a very busy man,' he said. Then, 'You will please come to the department. We must talk. I will be there at two o'clock.'

At two o'clock Professor R was not in the department and nobody in the outer office knew when or even whether he was likely to show up. I spent some time chatting with a pleasant American who turned out to be a visiting Fulbright professor – no, he hadn't seen Professor R either but as most of his salary was being paid for by the Fulbright Commission he wasn't under any financial strain – and then I tried Professor R's office once more.

'Enter.'

I entered. The man behind the desk looked like a cross between Aristotle Onassis and Tenniel's drawing of the frog footman. A mass of iron-grey hair combed back from his forehead. Thick, horn-rimmed spectacles, wide cheekbones, thick lips, and a retrousse chin. He was wearing a high-collared mustard-yellow shirt with a dark blue tie and a heavy black-and-white check sportscoat. The overall effect was of a '30s Hollywood producer blended with a shady dealer in second-hand cars. I introduced myself and, when it became apparent that he wasn't going to shake hands, looked round for a chair. The only one I could see was piled high with multiple copies of a book. I removed the books and sat down.

'I'm pleased we at last have the chance to talk,' I said.

He inclined his head, but whether in agreement I had no means of knowing. 'I must tell you that since we last communicated there have been some changes to our plans. It will not be possible for you to teach Shakespeare.' He paused, looked down at the hands folded in front of him, then said, 'The gentleman who usually teaches Shakespeare was greatly offended when I explained to him that you had asked to teach the Shakespeare course.'

'But I didn't ask,' I said. 'You asked *me.*'

Professor R paid no attention to my words. 'Therefore,' he said, 'I have arranged for you to teach the Romantics course.'

I was furious. For months I'd been preparing a series of classes on Shakespeare, and now, quite suddenly, and with the new academic year almost on us, I was being told to prepare for an entirely different course. It wasn't that I objected to lecturing on poets whose work I knew well, some of whom I'd written about, and most of whom I revered, but I didn't see why this change of plans should be foisted on me so abruptly and without so much as a by-your-leave.

'When was this known?' I asked. 'When did your Shakespeare colleague tell you he was displeased at the news I was to teach his course?'

'When – I – told – him – it – was – to – be – so,' Professor R said, as though explaining to a child that water is wet.

'Yes, but *when?*'

No reply.

'I can't say I think this a very courteous way of behaving,' I said. 'Surely once you knew the position you could have told me. As it is,

I have a few days at most to prepare an entirely different course from the one I assumed I'd be giving. When does teaching start, by the way?'

'You will be told.'

'Why can't I be told now? Don't you yourself know?'

Professor R breathed heavily. 'I am a very busy man,' he said.

In the months to come I would learn that this was his mantra for dodging answers to any questions he couldn't be bothered with and for exonerating himself from responsibility for not having done that which he ought to have done or for having done that which he ought not to have done. For example, after I happened upon the woman in the flat above mine opening my mail, I suggested to correspondents that in future they should direct all communications to my university address. A week later, when I went into the department, I found that all the letters and a parcel in my pigeon-hole had been opened and that on each was scrawled 'Opened in error. M R.' (Marius was Professor R's first name.) Enraged, I marched to his office and for once found him in situ. I threw the letters and parcel down on his desk. 'How can these have been opened in error?' I shouted. 'Every one of them is clearly addressed to me.'

'I am a very busy man,' he said.

By then our relationship had deteriorated to the extent that we didn't even pretend to civility. But at this first meeting I assumed him to be a man of honour. Perhaps he genuinely didn't know when the academic year began? I had heard from George and others that the Ministry of Education was interventionist, even *dirigiste*, regularly laying down the law about who could be employed by the universities, prying into the nature of the courses, going so far as to decide which books would be supplied to students free of charge. Perhaps term dates were decided by Ministry officials who had yet to inform the university. I said, 'Well, I'd be grateful if you would be sure to let me know the starting date. I don't want to be taken by surprise.'

As before he inclined his head. He may have thought our interview, brief and unsatisfactory as it was, had ended. But I had other questions to ask. 'I take it there is a teaching text for this course on the Romantics?' And when he said nothing, I added, 'If not, I recommend the *Norton Anthology*.'

'I regret to say that is not available,' he said. I was going to tell him that the day before I had seen copies piled up in one of the city's major bookshops, but before I could do so he added, 'Fortunately my own anthology *is* available.' He pointed to the pile of books I'd removed from the chair on which I had been sitting. 'Please to take one with you, you will find it has all you need.'

I gathered in the top copy. 'And how many students will be on the course?'

'Sixty-eight.'

'Sixty-eight?' I was astonished by his confidence.

'Sixty-eight,' he repeated.

I stood and made for the door. 'One other question,' I said. 'When we corresponded earlier in the year about my visiting professorship you asked me to send information in order to process my papers and ensure that I was put on the university payroll. I take it the information arrived?'

The head was silently inclined.

'Because naturally I'm concerned about my salary. Am I to be paid in arrears? I recall a letter telling me that I would be deemed to have commenced my year from September 1st. Does this mean I can expect my first payment in a few days time?'

'I am a very busy man,' Professor R said.

In the event, I wasn't paid until December. Long before that, however, Professor R and I had ceased to be on speaking terms. The rot set in a few days after our first meeting. I had gone up to the department to meet the Fulbright Professor with whom it turned out I was sharing an office, and with whom I'd agreed to go for a drink. I found him in conversation with a woman who was introduced to me as Dr P. As we shook hands, she said, 'Well, I may say that you have caused me no end of trouble.'

Though she spoke mock-ruefully her words puzzled, even startled me. 'I have? How?'

'By dropping the Shakespeare course. I have been asked to take it on. And like you I am a nineteenth century specialist. I have much work to do to prepare for this course.'

'But… but,' I said, when I got my breath back, 'Professor R gave me to understand that the department's Shakespeare specialist –

I'm sure he said it was a man – had been upset when he learnt that I was to teach the course.' I paused, then added by way of exculpation, 'Anyway, the idea was never mine, you know, it was Professor R's. I'd assumed I would be asked to lecture on Dickens, perhaps, or some other nineteenth-century topic.'

'I wish you had been,' she said graciously. 'I would have liked to hear you lecture on the subject. But what is this talk about a "Shakespeare specialist"? There is no such person in the department.'

I had by then decided against using Professor R's anthology, less because of its eccentric choice of poems than for its Janet-and-John-like commentary. 'Wordsworth liked the countryside but Keats preferred the town,' one note began, before plunging downhill. And after what Dr P had told me, I felt no uneasiness about letting him know. I was damned if I'd let him line his pockets by getting the Ministry to buy bulk copies of his lousy book which would then be foisted onto the hapless students. I left a note, explaining that although I had found looking through the anthology instructive, the *Norton*, being more comprehensive, was my preferred choice. And it was, I added, very definitely available.

It wasn't, however, supplied to the students I met at the first lecture. Sixty-eight of them Professor R had told me to expect, but when I climbed to the fifth floor of the poorly converted hotel where the lectures were to be held, I found what seemed, at a glance, at least two hundred students trying to cram themselves into a room that could hold fewer than half that number. Aghast, I stood on the landing to watch the mass of writhing bodies until from the far side of the room came a kerfuffle followed by a series of wails.

I tried to peer into the room, but couldn't see beyond the nearest ruck of bodies. The wails had risen and were now assuming hysteric proportions.

'What's going on?' I asked a student who had been ejected from a scrum near the door.

'A window's fallen out,' he said.

'*What!*'

As he spoke, various other students emerged, panting and sweating, onto the landing where I stood, and I was able, just, to force my way in and over to the far side of the room. Sure enough, a window had fallen out. Not merely the window. The window frame itself had given way and was now lying on the ground, far below, surrounding a man who knelt, head in hands, while a woman applied a handkerchief to his forehead and others, grouped round him, variously crossed themselves or gazed up at us, their arms held high in gestures of tragic supplication. As we watched, the sounds of an ambulance neared and soon the man was lifted onto a stretcher and taken out of sight.

'My god,' I said to a young woman student standing at my elbow, 'this is terrible. What on earth will happen now?'

A shrug. 'Nothing,' she said, turning a pair of blue eyes on me. 'When the man recovers he will sue the university for causing him this accident, and the university will sue the government for not looking after this building, and the government will sue the man for being on this street. That is how it goes in Greece.'

So it did, although when I left Greece a year later the affair of the fallen window hadn't even reached court. Each of the various parties was still preparing its case. Now, as we backed away from the open space where the window had been, I asked her another question. 'Why are there so many students here? I was assured the number would be sixty-eight.'

She laughed at my innocence. 'That is because there are sixty-eight seats in the room.'

She proved to be right on that score, too. Moreover, the chairs, steel-framed, were bolted to the floor. 'That is to prevent them from being stolen,' a different student told me.

'Or thrown at lecturers,' her companion, a male, said.

For the rest of the afternoon the students and I, or anyway as many of them as could pack into the room, devised a scheme whereby I could teach all those who wanted to study the Romantic poets. And as most did, insisting on their right to take the course of their choice, we agreed that the only solution was for me to divide them into three lecture groups and then give the same lecture three times over. Though this trebled my teaching schedule, the plan worked out pretty well as far as the students were concerned. Somehow, they came to an agreement about who would come to the nine o'clock class, who would prefer the ten o'clock hour, and who couldn't possibly make it earlier than eleven o'clock. As for the afternoon sessions – the course was a twice-weekly one – these too resolved themselves peacefully, although the two o'clock class rarely began with more than half the allotted number of students in position, and the four o'clock one steadily emptied as the hour wore on and students took themselves off to prepare for evening work. Most seemed to have jobs serving in bars or shops or tavernas, or of course teaching at language schools. They were affable but in no way apologetic about their leave-taking.

They did, however, apologise for abandoning class whenever they were called out on protest marches. During the autumn this frequently happened. Marianthi, the student who had on that first afternoon explained to me how Greek law worked, was year representative of the student body. Virtually every week she would enter midway through my eleven o'clock class, apologise briefly and then, having taken up a position in front of me, tell the students they had to leave immediately. A march on the Ministry of Education had been planned and would be followed by a rally. One week the protest might be over grants, the next over lack of accommodation, or poor quality teaching, or the squalor of the lecture rooms (hear, hear), or the absence of a library. (The English department had a library, but it was always locked. There was no librarian and the only key-holder was, of course, Professor R, who was never around to open it. 'I am a very busy man.')

'Sorry about this,' the students would say, as they filed from our fifth-floor eyrie, 'but we will see you later at the Medusa.'

The Medusa was a nearby coffee bar which, as time went on, I took to frequenting after the morning's lectures, and where I would invariably be joined by students, especially if they had been on a march and were in need of refreshment. Not that they drank or ate much. For one thing they were, most of them, poor. For another, they got by with little need for liquid refreshment. A soft drink, a frappé, even a glass of water, hardly ever a beer, let alone wine: they would sit for hours with a half-empty glass in front of them, talking. Talking gave them the high that alcohol couldn't provide, and after a march there would be much to discuss. It appeared that most rallies ended with a further march to the American Hilton, where windows would be stoned and the Stars and Stripes burnt.

As the year advanced, I came to appreciate the reasons for my students' anti-Americanism. The junta had been backed by the CIA, American tanks – even though they were driven by the junta's soldiers – had been used to put down the student uprising of November 17th, 1973, and American air force bases in outer Athens were regarded as imperialistic impositions on a sovereign nation. Fair enough.

As to their anger at the university's – or was it the government's? – failure to provide the free course books which were routinely promised and as routinely failed to arrive, it was one I shared. My own course was in difficulties because we had no text the students could consult. Some time after I had left the note telling Professor R that I proposed to use the *Norton Anthology* and would need about two hundred copies of it, he had returned it to my pigeon-hole with the underlined message: 'Not Available.' This was followed by an equally emphatic message: 'MY ANTHOLOGY CAN BE READILY SUPPLIED.' Over my dead body, I thought.

What to do? I decided to type out poems on which I would base lectures and discussions, have them photocopied, and hand them out to the students. That at least would give us a minimal number of texts we could refer to in some detail.

I set to work, typed out some twenty poems of various lengths, took them into the department, and asked – begged – a secretary to make the necessary number of photocopies. The next day I found a note in my pigeon-hole, together with my typed-out poems. It read, 'Free photocopying is available only to permanent members of staff. M R.' I marched round to the nearest photocopying shop and spent nearly three hours in completing four thousand pages of photocopying. I then spent further hours stapling the collated pages together. The bill more or less cleaned me out. Mightily pleased all the same, I began the next lecture by handing out sixty sets of the photocopies, explained to the students in the class that as the university had not as yet paid me, and I was therefore short of funds, I would be grateful if each of them would pay one hundred drachms to recover the cost of my photocopying labours.

They were polite but firm. They had been promised free books and free books they would have. The photocopied sheets were rejected.

Now what? I decided to follow the example set by William Empson when, in the Far East and a long way from any library, he taught from memory, writing on the blackboard poems to which his students had no other access. I have a strong memory and for a while it was fun to write out poems that the students could then copy down – although most complained that my handwriting, with which I took great pains, was illegible, and others that their chairs were bolted to the floor in positions, behind pillars, they meant, from which it was impossible to see the blackboard. Still, we just about managed until one day I went in and found that the box containing chalks had disappeared. Rumours of Professor R having been seen scurrying from the building shortly before my lecture began were probably well-founded.

One day in early November I went into the office I shared with my Fulbright colleague. He was backed up against the wall by a student I didn't recognise who was plainly in a rage and, it seemed, on the edge of violence. As I approached, the student backed off, shook his fist at us both, then turned abruptly away.

I waited until he had slammed out of the room before asking, 'What on earth was that about?'

'Jeez!' He sat, took some deep breaths and shook his head in wonderment. 'What a setup. The guy was complaining that I'd given him a lower grade than his friend.'

'But why get so worked up about it? I thought he was going to thump you.'

'So did I.' He took some more breaths, then explained that the paper in question was a re-sit from the previous year's examinations, and that the student, who moments before had been at his throat, having along with several others failed the examination in American literature, had been required to re-sit it in September. 'But get this. I didn't even grade the damned papers.' That, apparently, had been the duty of the previous Fulbright professor, a duty he had carried out just prior to leaving.

'And Mr Nice Guy failed again?'

'No, he passed.'

'Then why,' I asked, 'the fuss?'

'Because he got a five and his friend got a seven.'

65

'And male vanity was at stake. He won't be the first man in the world to think himself at least the equal of all others.'

He laughed. 'No, it's not that. Seems he and his friend wrote identical answers, word for word. So if one gets seven, the other should get seven.'

'You mean they cheated? Well, then, they should both get nought.'

'Trouble is, they don't see it that way.' And then, as I opened my mouth to reply, he said, 'Look, I could use a drink, you care to join me?'

A few minutes later, installed over a jug of retsina at the Medusa – which at this time of morning we had more or less to ourselves – I learnt something of the lengths Greek students would as a matter of course go to in order to ensure academic success. Copying each others' essays was the least of it. They would offer to bribe their lecturers (though I don't think the American 'A for a lay' was often used); they would invent the most elaborate explanations for failure to hand in work – these usually began with the illness or death of a grandmother and continued with further family bereavements and disasters until, sometimes after enough deaths to fill a necropolis, they were granted a reprieve; they even leaned on friends and 'cousins' working in examination offices to alter the grades that had to be centrally recorded. 'So when you fill in exam registers make sure you give the grades in letters as well as numbers,' I was told. 'Altering a two to an eight is easy. It's done all the time.'

'How do you know all this?' I asked. 'Did Professor R treat you to a complete account of student corruption? Or did he make you buy his book on the subject?'

'One of the lecturers in the department filled me in. Nice woman. Teaches with me on the American literature course. Have you met her?' But the name he offered meant nothing to me, nor did I expect it to. 'I know hardly anyone here,' I said. 'Nobody has so much as asked me to go for a cup of coffee. And as for a meeting of minds...'

'That's the way it is. Soon as they've done teaching they're off to their language schools.'

'I thought that was outlawed.'

'So's cheating. But like I say, they don't think of it as we do. It's more a form of haggling. Some you win, some you lose. Either way, no hard feelings.'

I re-filled our glasses. 'That student who was with you half an hour ago seemed to be taking his grade pretty hard.'

'He'll be OK by now,' he said, and, as a way of putting the subject behind him, asked me if I'd been paid yet. No, I told him, and he shook his head in disbelief.

It might have been two weeks later that we were in the office when a smart-looking Greek woman entered. 'My colleague, Dr C,' he said, introducing us to each other. She was wearing a beige-coloured skirt and jacket over a white ruffled blouse, and told us she was on her way to supervise the last hour of a mid-term examination of third-year students. Would I like to go with her? Afterwards, we might perhaps have lunch together. As this was the first time I'd had the chance to meet any lecturer in the department, or in any other department for that matter, I readily agreed.

'Though I have to be back for my two o'clock class,' I said.

'Ah, the two o'clock class. Followed by the three o'clock class and then the four o'clock class. I have heard of you. We think you must be mad to make such work for yourself.' Her laugh revealed a set of even, gleaming white teeth. My guess that she'd spent years living in America – those teeth, so unlike the tobacco-stained and chipped teeth of most Greeks, had surely been achieved by expensive dentistry – was confirmed by her telling me as we walked to an adjacent building that both her first and second degrees came from the University of Chicago, 'which I loved.'

'So why did you come back?'

'Love again. My husband was Greek. He wanted to return to Athens.'

'Was?'

'We are divorced. Now, here we are.'

'Here' was the department of law, the only building, so she explained, with a room large enough to accommodate the three hundred students sitting this particular linguistics examination. We climbed a staircase, went along a corridor whose every inch of wall was lined with torn posters, most of them superimposed on other torn posters, and then, motioned through a door by Dr C, I found myself at the back of a raked lecture theatre. Below, in tiered rows, students sat shoulder to shoulder, writing, and while she made her way down to the front to relieve a female colleague who had been acting as invigilator, I sat down in the back, unoccupied row, and I let my eye wander over the scene.

At first I could hardly believe what I was seeing. This was cheating on an industrial scale. Moreover, it was entirely without any attempt at a cover-up. Pieces of paper were being passed from hand to hand, along rows, across rows, from front to back. Students leaned over to check each others' papers, offer whispered comments, suggest revisions, nod in confirmation, shrug in response to enquiries they couldn't answer. Dr C must surely have been aware of at least some of this, but the only occasions on which she lifted her head from the book she had fished out of her bag, and was now reading attentively, were when a candidate requested more paper or begged a glass of water from one of the several carafes on the examiner's desk. Sometimes, when the whisperings grew to be more like the sound of a mighty, rushing wind, she frowned, but as that died away her face cleared, and she would return to her book.

When the hour was finally up, she stood, announced that the examination was at an end, that students must cease immediately, and, sure enough, ten or so minutes later most of the students finished what they were writing. Then, having gathered up their bags, pens, pencils and papers, they slowly left the room, many of the women students hand in hand, the men with arms round each others' shoulders.

I helped Dr C gather the examination scripts together. 'Are these to be locked away for safekeeping?' I asked as we piled them onto the desk at which she had sat.

She smiled at my innocence. 'Someone will be along soon to collect them. We are free to go now.'

Over lunch I mentioned the pieces of paper I had seen the students passing back and forth. Had she been aware of what they were doing? Oh, yes. 'They call them *skournakis*. After the paper in which apothecaries would wrap pills or powder. I have seen some, no bigger than the palm of your hand, on which were written hundreds of words. And I have been told that one is in circulation that contains two thousand words. *Two thousand.*

Can you imagine?' Her eyes glinted with what seemed amused pride.

'And you knew that they were cheating?'

'Of course.'

'And it doesn't worry you?'

She shrugged. 'Look. Students at the University of Athens are given a bad time. Their lecturers – most of them anyway – take no interest in them, the system sucks them in and then spews them out, so why shouldn't they be as cynical as those who run that system?'

'Would you say that of all students? I mean, suppose some cheat their way through medicine or let's say civil engineering. I wouldn't feel too good if I knew I was driving across a bridge that had been built by someone with an unearned qualification.'

She shook her head vehemently. 'That would not happen,' she said, 'our engineers are among the best in the world. And our doctors. As for the students in the English department, they are right to despise this examination system. It exists not to help them but for the convenience of those who cannot be bothered to teach them properly. And you know,' she paused, looked at me as though expecting my approval, 'they cheat co-operatively. They help each other. In America, I knew some students who cheated, and most of them did it so as to show themselves better than other students. They wanted to "steal a march" on them, I think you say. That is not so here.'

'The same grade for the same work,' I said.

'Exactly.' She held her glass aloft and we clinked and drank.

'And what's the lowest pass mark?'

'Five,' she said. 'Five is what you need to stay alive.'

A few days after that lunchtime conversation, George phoned me at the department. 'John, you know I disapprove of cheating.' This was a reference to a discussion of the previous evening, where over food and drink I had reported my astounded discovery of the lengths to which cheating in the English department at Athens could go.

'Yes.'

'Yes. However, my head of department is very concerned in case his mistress has not passed her examination.' George went on to explain that the woman in question, whose name he slowly spelt out, having the previous year enrolled for courses in the university's English department, had failed a crucial examination which she had been obliged to re-sit, and she was now worried that she might have failed the re-sit paper. 'And if so, she must leave the university. And this will be very bad for her career.'

'And how am I supposed to help?' I took for granted help was what was expected of me. 'I have nothing to do with the first year courses.'

Speaking very carefully, George said, 'You can perhaps discover whether she has scored a five. FIVE. *FIVE*. It is very important that she scores five. FIVE. *FIVE*. That is the number she must score. FIVE.'

'I think I understand,' I said.

And George, indifferent to my irony, said, 'Good. Because if she has scored five – *FIVE* – my head of department will be extremely grateful to you. *FIVE*.' And he broke the connection.

Given all that I'd seen on the morning of the linguistics examination, and all that I'd been told, I wondered how any student in the English department could ever fail an examination. Ah, well, perhaps this particular paper had been taken by someone unpopular with other students, who wouldn't therefore let her have access to the mobile library of *skournakis*. Or maybe her paper had been marked by someone unaware of how the system worked. Right both times. I made enquiries and found that the woman student was widely disliked for her arrogant disregard of others, and that the original paper had been assessed by a newly-appointed part-time lecturer, an American who had previously taught in Japan, where the integrity of the examination system was taken for granted.

I hunted him down, and after introducing myself, asked whether as a matter of interest he could tell we whether Miss B, whose re-sit paper I understood him to have marked, had managed to pass. I was enquiring, I explained, for a friend, who took some interest in her. He looked at me speculatively, then shuffled through his papers, and finally told me that yes, he had found it in his heart to give the dumb cluck a mark of five. 'So your friend can rest easy.'

I went back to my office and phoned George. 'She passed,' I said. 'She got five.'

'That is very, *very* good,' George said. He sounded both relieved and mightily pleased. 'I will tell my head of department. I can tell you that he will be very grateful.'

The next morning, after I'd finished my classes, and before heading for the Medusa, I dropped into the department, hoping against hope that someone from Finance might have left a note telling me that at last the salary I was owed was available for collection. Nothing doing. But as I was turning away from my pigeon-hole the American (whose mark of five to an undeserving case had presumably safeguarded the love life of George's boss) hailed me from his open office door.

'Come over here,' he said.

I went over and he stood aside to usher me into his room. 'Just take a look at this.'

'This' was a large cardboard box, open on the uncarpeted floor of his office. Inside I could see bottles. He drew one out. Black label Johnnie Walker. He gave it to me. 'Go on, have it, there are eleven more where that came from. Know why?'

I stared at him with a wild surmise. 'You tell me.'

'Dr T. Friend of the woman you were asking about yesterday. He must have thought I fixed her mark. So I get a case of Johnnie Walker for doing my duty.'

He showed me the label that had been tucked inside the box. 'With grateful thanks, GT.'

'Such, my son, are the rewards of virtue.' His eyes brimmed with unholy laughter.

That evening George called to say that Dr T and his girlfriend, both of them determined to show gratitude for my part in what they assumed was the 'arrangement' by which her pass mark had been manufactured, proposed to take the two of us out for a slap-up meal. The following night, therefore, we were driven in Dr T's Mercedes to a flunky-infested restaurant at Kifissia (the poshest of Athens's suburbs, where the houses are the size of Belgravia mansions and exclusively occupied by millionaire bankers and top government officials), and for several hours poked about among poor, imitation French dishes while listening to talk of such mind-rotting banality that I positively ached for Babi's. The only remark of hers I can recall was one to the effect that Geneva, where the pair of them had been the previous weekend, was a dull city. 'There was nothing to do, so I put on my fur coat and walked up and down.'

And then, at the very end of the evening, she momentarily flickered into life. By then they were both drunk and she made a slighting reference to the wife whom he kept at home but rarely saw.

'I don't like the way you talk,' he told her.

'Really?' she said. 'Well, I don't like the way you fuck.'

November became December. The days shortened, though they continued warm enough for me to sit out at my favourite bar in the Plaka, where, still unpaid by the university, I had now to watch my drachms. Some students found me there one lunchtime after I'd spent the morning working in the British Council library. The previous evening, they told me, they had seen on TV reports of the miners' strike. 'It was terrible,' one said, looking at me in wonderment. 'England is like Greece used to be.'

'How do you mean?'

'A police state. The police, they jump out of vans, and they beat the miners, then they take them to prison.'

I began to defend my country. To be sure, I was on the miners' side, but I couldn't accept that England was a police state, although TV could of course sensationalise events, and there was no doubt that Thatcher encouraged bully-boy tactics. But the students' vehemence both alarmed me – perhaps matters had taken a sudden turn for the worse since I had last read an English newspaper – and then, as they talked on, alerted me to something I hadn't before considered: that Greece had access to uncut film of what was happening on the picket lines in the UK. That evening I went to a student apartment and a group of us watched as well-drilled ranks of policemen used dogs and horses to assist in their baton-charging of the miners. Afterwards I spoke by phone to Pauline. It soon became apparent that she hadn't access to the half of what I had been looking at, and that British TV, even Channel 4, was censoring reports, with the result that viewers in the UK were fed anodyne, misleading and, to all intents and purposes, lying accounts of what in fact was taking place in mining districts. It wasn't the miners who were attacking the police, for

God's sake. The police were attacking the miners, safe in the knowledge that whatever they did had government backing.

I reported my conversation to the students. See, they said, we were right. Well, no, I said, England still had a free press. The students looked doubtful. Then they did something lovely. At the very last class before the Christmas break, and knowing that the following day I would be flying home for three weeks, they came crowding into the lecture room to present me with three thousand drachms they had collected for the miners' families.

'You will give the money to them from us,' they said, handing over the money together with a large card onto which well over a hundred signatures and messages of support had, in true *skournaki* style, been crammed. Three thousand drachms was worth about ten pounds, but it had been collected by students who for the most part had damn all money to spare.

'Of course I will,' I said, touched by their warmth and generosity. Then, having agreed to meet them later for one last drink at the Medusa, I went back to my office to be greeted by the Fulbright professor. He was grinning. 'Guess what,' he said, 'it's Christmas and I've just heard news. We're gonna be paid.'

'You're kidding.'

'Nope. Gospel truth. Got a phone call half an hour ago. Course the news isn't as important to me, Athens is only paying a quarter of my salary, but I can do with the money, so let's go down together.' Which was what we did.

An hour and a half later, the two of us emerged from the university treasury into the streets of Athens, our wallets, our pockets, our socks, even our underpants, crammed with banknotes. Because, when we presented ourselves on the fourth floor of the correct building (building, floor and then room had all taken some finding) we were told by the slump-shouldered official who eventually looked up from the desk before which we stood in eager expectancy, that the university did not issue cheques to its employees and we would therefore be paid in cash. I was, he told me, owed 498,000 drachm. From a drawer in his desk, the official produced an enormous wad of notes and slowly, pausing every so often to lick forefinger and thumb, and rather more frequently to draw on the cigarette propped in his overflowing ashtray, began to count out a sequence of one thousand drachm notes, all the way from one to 498.

Slowly, slowly, the pile of bank notes grew.

'496, 497, 498.' But wait. An additional fifty-eight loose drachms had to be added. More rummaging in his desk-drawer before these could be found. I made to reach for the pile. Aha, not so fast. Before I could pocket the money, I had first to re-count every note to ensure that he had dispensed the correct amount, after which I had to sign, and only after that could I scoop up the cash I was owed.

'Look,' I said, 'I'm prepared to take the risk that there's 498,000 drachms here.'

Oh, no. His reputation was at stake. Very well, let him have it his way.

Pretending to count in multiples of ten, I completed what I announced was a tally of 498,000 drachms. Honour finally satisfied, I bundled the notes into my leather shoulder bag and, wishing the man *kronia pola*, got out of the room as quickly as I could.

On the stairs I felt the Fulbright professor's hand on my shoulder. 'You go out on the streets like that,' he said, 'you're sure to be mugged.'

'Mugged? In Athens? Oh, come on. I've walked the streets of this city at all hours of day and night' – I had, too – 'and I've never felt threatened, not once. Athens is the safest city in the world. There's nothing to worry about.'

'You've not been threatened because you've never had money on you. A mugger can *smell* money, believe me. You don't spread the money you've got about you and you'll end up in real trouble.'

And so, partly to play along with his conviction that Syntagma and Times Squares were one and the same thing, and partly because his nervousness had got to me, I did as he suggested, made small bundles of the 498 notes and distributed them about my body.

And a few minutes later we were walking up Akademias Street, at each step crackling like cellophane. Never mind the smell, hear the noise.

But I made it unscathed to the Medusa, where a larger than usual group of students was already seated. 'Guess what,' I said. 'It's Christmas. I've been paid and the drinks are on me.' There were cheers and some applause.

I ordered for everyone and from the depths of my being – my armpit, actually – produced a one thousand drachm note. 'Hey presto.'

The young woman serving us shook her head. 'No change,' she said, 'do you have something smaller?' And of course I hadn't. Just 497 more of the same.

The Taverna on Filis Street

'who so willing may go in, for there is nothing within the
house that is private of anie man's own.'
SIR THOMAS MORE, UTOPIA

The blind man scrapes his stringless violin,
whistles, and a grin buffs his cheeks as George
folds drachs into his pocket. When he leaves
grizzled *bousoukia* players start to sing

'*s'agapo*'. Tonight's special is a Delphic treat:
'for you, Mister John, to give you strength in love'.
And Babi's wily fingers prise from a sheep's cracked skull
white, wrinkled pulp. 'Is good, I tell you. Eat.'

In go the bent tin forks. Dimitris, Manos, Aleka,
Fotini, Anna, friends and friends of friends: tonight
and every night all seats are taken, yet still
Babi finds space for others. 'Come in, sit here.'

Talk crams between the anyhow tumblers, plates,
brimming copper jugs, and a lottery-ticket seller
empties my glass, though the barrel's resined flow
won't stop. So, welcome one more *miso*! – 'to brush your teeth'.

S'*agapo*. And Babi's winey breath
blesses the tables of the true Demos…

And in London, at tables round which maids
flicker silent as shadows, united
by the dividing salt, monogrammed soup spoons
dip and rise, desirable as AIDS.

CHAPTER FOUR

At Babi's

I'T'S FRIDAY, TEN PM. Dimitris, Elias and I have just met George, who's come bustling up Acharnon Street from his language school, and after the obligatory handshakes and kisses we head for the taverna on Filis Street. *Taverna ta Spata* is painted over its green door – green for a taverna that cooks meat, blue for fish – but everyone knows it as Babi's. Babi comes from a village near Spata and tonight, as every night except Monday, he is open for business. Ten o'clock being early for Friday night habitués, the taverna is only half full and we therefore have several tables to choose between. I suggest one near the back wall, Dimitris then proposes one in the middle, Elias indicates his preference for one nearer the exit, and George, after a good deal of speculative consideration, finger under chin, eye in a fine frenzy rolling, decides that we should sit at a table close to the barrels.

Ah, the barrels. There are four of them, racked up on sturdy shelf beams that run from the far end of the inner wall to the opening beyond which, in the kitchen, Babi's mother and (sometimes) a cousin prepare and cook food that has, nearly all of it, come from Babi's home village, where his family has lived for generations. The barrels are enormous: wide and deep enough, I think, to drown whole armies of Clarences, and they contain the best retsina in the world. It, too, comes from Babi's native village, and because we are trusties, as soon as we arrive one or other of us is permitted to fill a copper jug from whichever barrel Babi gestures towards and to collect glasses from the high counter separating the kitchen area from the rest of the taverna. It may take some time before Babi is free to come to our table, but we are not required to wait for drink. And so we clink our filled glasses, bang them on the table, wish ourselves and everyone else good health, and take our first sips.

'Tonight, it is very good,' George announces, his voice blending surprise and gratification, as though the retsina might have been other than wonderful, which it never is. I love the slightly salty, brackish flavour, and when I hold it up for inspection the wine's honey-yellow seems filled with Greek sunlight. And so cheap! A litre jug costs about forty drachms, which translates to something like fifteen pence. 'A man might drown in claret before he would be drunk on it,' Dr Johnson famously said. I have no intention of becoming drunk on retsina, but I sometimes feel I could swim in a sea of it and not count the cost. And certainly before the night is done we will have re-filled our jug more times than anyone, including Babi, can count. Not that this bothers him. When the time comes to pay, he will write out our bill on a corner of the paper tablecloth, make a guess as to how much we have drunk, tear the bill off and with a flourish lay it down in front of one of us, usually accompanying it with a last half-litre of wine. 'To brush your teeth,' he says. I never know whether the amount we pay is an accurate reflection of what we have eaten and drunk, but do know that it seems hardly to vary between evenings when we have ordered little and those when we have stuffed ourselves, but I would willingly pay far more than I ever do for the joy the taverna unfailingly brings me.

As now, when Dimitris is trying to tell us a joke about a professor and a frog. 'So the professor, he cut off the frog's last leg and he say "jump" but the frog he does not move. And the professor he tells his students, "so you see, when we cut off all a frog's legs he become deaf".' I think it quite a good joke but George is not listening. That Babi has not yet come to tell us what he has on offer this evening, but is instead loitering to talk to the occupants of other tables, causes George some concern. 'Grub before ethics' – George would modify Brecht's motto to 'grub before anything.' Now, as Babi heads in our direction, George relaxes. Babi arrives at our table, shakes hands with each of us, then announces, 'Tonight I have…' and there follows a long list of salads, vegetable dishes, pasta, meat – chops, steaks, stews – delivered with a suave assurance that we know better than to interrupt. Once he has finished, there is much discussion as to what each will have for second plates, the first plates – salads, vegetables – being communal. I rarely bother with the details of ordering: whatever Babi chooses to bring will suffice. Anyway, he never writes our orders down, and although he rarely makes a mistake one of us has occasionally to make do with, say, a pork steak rather than the stuffed aubergines. The friable corn bread, with its aroma of dill seed, that, like the retsina, comes endlessly to the table, the knowledge that we can sit here for hours without being pestered by waiters routinely anxious to clear used plates ('everything to your satisfaction, sir?'), the sense that the evening will proceed at a pace whose rhythms are not determined by external considerations – this is paradise enough.

Now George is leading us through an account of the previous day's gastric discomforts. 'At college,' – the academy where he teaches each morning and for which he routinely leaves home at six-thirty – 'I was feeling a little hungry. So I had some bars of chocolate and a cheese pie. Then, when I got home, father had prepared some pasta which I ate, although I was a little hungry still so I had another pie. Then, I had a siesta. Then, when I woke, I ate the rest of the pasta which father had put in the fridge. Then my stomach started to ache' – he rubs his belly vigorously – 'so I drank a little brandy.' He tilts his head back, and pours invisible drink down his opened mouth. 'Then I went to the *frontisterion*' – his own language school – 'but I was still a little hungry' – more palpating his belly – 'so I sent one of the boys out for a pie. Then, when I got home, I had a steak and then my stomach felt bad again so I had some more brandy.' A sigh and a shake of the head. 'I don't know. Perhaps I should see a doctor.'

As he says this, food begins to arrive at our table: a large bowl of Greek salad, a plate of small cheese pies, one of green beans, another of fried, thin-sliced courgettes, two of chips, and at once George takes up a fork and begins to stab avidly at the pies while Dimitris and I, picking more sparingly among green beans, courgettes, and fried cheese, hear out Elias's story. It concerns Elias's attempt to convince his class (like George, Elias teaches at the Academy) that the ancient Spartans, though on average no more than five feet high, each carried three hundred pounds of armour and weaponry into battle with them. 'Imagine,' he says to me, 'so strong, those men.' A pause. 'By the way, John, how do you know when an Englishwoman wants you to take your hand off her thigh?' For Elias cannot understand why Englishwomen aren't as free with their sexual favours as all his friends assure him they've found them to be. Why else, after all, should such women come to Greece? On a previous occasion he has told me, in puzzlement, that he had a few days earlier fallen into conversation with an Englishwoman and that he was sure she was interested in him. So he asked for her telephone number, but instead she got him to give her his, and promised to ring him. 'But she has not done so,' he said. 'Perhaps she has lost my number.'

'Perhaps she has,' I said.

And now, as other plates arrive, and as Dimitris cuts his steak into pieces and out of natural generosity and hospitable intent offers each of us a morsel – 'this is very delicious' – and George prongs a lamb cutlet, and Elias the *karkarias*, slim in electric-blue shirt and too-white, too-tight trousers, picks reflectively at his food – I can look at my companions and around at other tables which are being taken by couples, groups, whole families from babies to the ancient of days, and, aware of the constant wash of talk and laughter, of the aromas that pass us as Babi brings armfuls of food to waiting customers who are also, for the most part, friends, can raise my glass in yet another toast to everyone present tonight and think truly that there is nowhere else I would rather be, and wish that my English friends and my family could be here to share in this earthly delight.

It was Pauline who'd spotted Babi's taverna. Not long before she left Athens, and nursing her broken wrist, she'd been wandering the backstreets near the flat on Acharnon Street when she came upon a whitewashed single-storey building, one of the older sort that still survive in Athens among all the ghastly and not so ghastly apartment blocks. Taverna ta Spata, 120 Filis Street, wasn't yet open for the season – like many tavernas at that time Babi's closed during the summer – but, noticing that the door was ajar, she peered in. A man was sweeping the floor, another was unstacking chairs, and she could hear a clatter of pans coming from what had to be the kitchen area. A tap on her shoulder and she turned to find herself confronted by a burly, middle-aged man with grey eyes and what could have been a broken nose. He looked like a genial ex-pugilist, would in earlier times have been called a fine figure of a man, and although she didn't then know it she was looking at Babi. Might he know when the taverna planned to open, she asked in English, and in English the man replied, 'October.'

'You'll have to try it' she told me when she returned from her walk, 'it looks your sort of place.' I knew I could trust her. Some fifteen years earlier, when we arrived in Beeston, that part of outer Nottingham where we still live, Pauline had been cycling up a side-street when she'd passed a small pub called The Royal Oak. As she would later do at Babi's, she took it upon herself to peer inside, then came back home and told me about it. 'It's your kind of a pub,' she said, and it was. From then on, at all events until the policy of the brewery that owned the pub dictated it be gutted and turned into a ridiculous barn of a place, The Royal Oak became my version of The Moon in the Water. The beer was always well-kept and the two front rooms, bar to left, lounge to right, were home to 'plain ordinary folk' as well as a gaggle of wondrous eccentrics. Among my favourites was one known as Sheffield Tommy, a very short man with a battered, shiny face, two inverted commas for a nose, and a fine line in porkpie hats, who according to his own account had fed Churchill a meal from his desert canteen when the war leader had visited the Eighth Army – ' "Burton", Churchill said to me, "Burton, if we had more like you this war would have been won by now" ' – and who, when he received his weekly wages for dishwashing chores at the university, spent them out on Friday nights in The Oak, where he entertained the punters to endless renditions of 'Roses of Picardy', 'I Believe' and 'There'll be Bluebirds over the White Cliffs of Dover', performances which despite his undeniably resonant bel canto, failed to delight successive landlords, all of whom nursed a belief that if it weren't for the likes of Sheffield Tommy the pub might cater to the carriage trade. Fanatics have their dreams.

Not that these dreams led to any broadening of the pub's drinks policy. Beer and basic spirits were on offer. If you wanted anything fancier, you went elsewhere. I once took to The Oak a friend who had on his arm a home counties girlfriend. What would she like to drink? She asked for a sherry. 'Sherry?' the landlord of the moment yelped. Then, recovering his poise, 'What kind of sherry? Red or brown?'

Yet in earlier times, the pub had made much of Saturday lunchtimes, when the nearby lace factories finished for the weekend. Workers coming off duty donned black bow ties and bowlers and made for The Oak's small back room, known as the Snug, where they downed Guinness and oysters. That routine, along with the lace factories themselves, had ceased by the time I made The Oak my regular watering-hole, but still on Friday nights a man in a white coat carrying a wicker basket would go from room to room selling shellfish brought straight, so he said, from Grimsby. And there would be an air of gaiety about the place that was intensified not merely by Sheffield Tommy's singing but by the appearance of various other entertainers, most notably an old man who came in mid-evening accompanied by his wife, and who for his party trick would at random pick up someone's half-filled glass, order someone else to hand over a coin, throw the coin into the glass and then beckon it to come out, which it unfailingly did. For an encore he would borrow a lit cigarette, remove his cap, put the cigarette in his cap, invert it, and the cigarette would crawl out from underneath and come to rest on his cap's peak. It was the most spectacular feat of legerdemain I've ever witnessed, done in full view of people crowded all around, and, beyond drinking the contents of the glass he had borrowed and smoking the rest of the cigarette, he would take no reward. The coin was always returned to its owner.

Years later, when I met him one day in the street, he explained how he used cat gut with a dob of glue, and he showed me the callus on his finger about which the cat gut was wound. His wife was dead, he told me, and he himself now suffered from arthritic joints and could no longer work the trick, but he seemed remarkably un-self-pitying.

Simple Simon was also without self-pity. Not much taller than Sheffield Tommy, Simon wore a succession of brightly-checked sportscoats that were far too large for him, had a grin as wide as George Formby's, and invariably arrived in the pub with a suitcase full of clothes – shirts, socks, underwear – which he insisted a friend had given him to sell. 'He'd be here himself, but he's indisposed.'

Simon rarely managed to sell much before the arrival of a policeman put an end to his trade.

'Thought I might find you here, Simon. What you got in that suitcase?'

'I'm just going on holiday, officer.'

'You are indeed, Simon.'

And off Simon would go, to be detained for a few months at her majesty's pleasure, sometimes in Lincoln Gaol, more often at the

Open Prison at Oakham, where he contentedly helped look after the garden and in season played football – 'If you're ever sent there, John, ask to play in goal. Gives you time to look around, there's some smashing scenery' – and kept an obliging eye on more troubled inmates. 'You get some right weirdos, ones that don't know what's good for them. Tryin' to scarper, can you believe it?'

The pub also played host to Dennis and Doreen, a couple who after their day's work, he as brickie, she as general char, made straight for The Oak, aiming to arrive as the doors opened for business. Once inside, they would stand silently at the bar until each had downed a third glass – Dennis drank pints of Guinness while Doreen's tipple was rum and coke – at which point they would become suddenly and in Dennis's case confusingly eloquent. Dennis spoke in tongues. At all events, nobody had the faintest idea what he was talking about, not even Doreen, who simply ignored him. Not that it mattered. If a remark was addressed to you as you stood at the bar waiting to be served, you had simply to agree or, if it seemed more appropriate, nod in grave silence.

'Hoo hammer sill untro wilter.'

'Dead right, Dennis. Couldn't have put it better myself.'

This went on until, towards the end of the evening, Doreen, skirt now hitched high over laddered stockings, chose to canter unsteadily from room to room in the fond belief, so legend had it, that she was providing her audience with a plausible imitation of Old Mother Riley. The conclusion of her nightly ritual was the signal for Dennis, who had by now downed at least eight pints of Guinness and resumed his silent reign, to keel rigidly over, from which prone position he would be lifted onto the shoulders of his mate, a woman far stronger than her stick-like figure suggested, and hauled from The Oak while conversation proceeded as usual. 'Same time tomorrow night,' Doreen would shout, as the front door swung shut behind them both. 'Aye, see you,' Chris, or Derek, or Norman, those successive landlords, would call.

Imagine Dennis and Doreen at Babi's. Well, why not? At his taverna they would have sat and eaten their fill, whereas The Oak, as with most spit-and-sawdust pubs, provided no more by way of evening food than whatever filled cobs were left over from the lunchtime trade, plus pickled eggs rumoured to survive within the murky liquid that filled a large jar standing for years on the bar until someone finally threw it out. But would Dennis and Doreen have wanted to eat at Babi's? Most assuredly, yes. Because all were welcomed at Taverna ta Spata, the farmer and the clown, the poorest he and she. You might desire or be able to afford no more than a glass of retsina and a piece of bread, but you would be received as hospitably as anyone ordering plate after plate of the taverna's fresh-cooked food.

'What's posh?' my friend Matt Simpson asked me in rhetorical wonderment when, years later, he sat with me at a backstreet taverna on Aegina and watched as people at neighbouring tables applied cheap tin utensils to food that was served on cheap white plates, and poured retsina from cheap copper tankards into cheap tumblers, all the while exchanging friendly banter with the taverna owner and his family and talking and laughing unconstrainedly as they ate, often wandering from table to table to greet friends or renew acquaintance. Some of the clients may have been wealthy, others were undeniably poor. But all were equally welcome, nobody was made to 'feel out of place', to use the phrase that tells you so much about the codes of speech, of dress, of behaviour, that infect our still class-ridden society.

'What's posh?' Not Babi's taverna, for sure. The first time I was there, a middle-aged, distinguished-looking man, dressed in check sportscoat and grey trousers with well-polished black shoes, made his way to our table and, speaking some words I didn't understand, shook hands with George, then with me. He was carrying an attaché-case, and from his lean, keen-eyed face, the trim but ample moustache and neatly cut hair, I judged him to be a fellow teacher. After some minutes' conversation with George he opened his attaché-case and George opened his wallet. The man was selling lottery tickets.

There were occasions – not many, but there were some – when I went to Babi's alone. On such occasions I'd take a book with me, intending to while away the hours in contented isolation. But my plan never worked out. Always, I would be summoned by the occupants of a nearby table and invited to eat and drink with them. To have said that I preferred my own company would have been impossible, inconceivable. If I wanted to be on my own, why come to a taverna? And as I didn't want to affront or insult Greek hospitality, I did as I was asked to do. In his novel *Father Dancing*, Nick Papandreou remarks that there is no Greek word for isolation. Not true, but I can understand his point. Isolation or solitariness is undesirable, it implies a failure of hospitality, since nobody can wish to live in isolation. It follows that nobody can or should be left to their own devices. Greek friends were appalled when they heard from me of old people in England being found dead in their own flats or houses, sometimes weeks after they had died. This happened not infrequently during the prolonged cold spell of the winter of 1984–5, usually because the gas or electricity supply had been cut off, or because, fearing they hadn't the wherewithal to pay, old-age pensioners would simply not risk using the only means they had to keep themselves warm. 'Such a thing could not happen here,' George said, and I thought of the old woman who was to be seen, every Sunday, sitting on an upturned orange crate in the street where he lived, waiting for the dinner which people took it in turns to bring to her.

Kindness to strangers operated not merely in tavernas and on the streets of Athens. Whenever in later years I went for an early morning swim from Aegina's town beach, my hopes of finding and keeping a spot to myself were always scuppered. Early morning was the time when a group of old ladies would come down to the beach. Later in the day would be too hot, and anyway they had household duties. 'The Hattery' I called that group of ordinary dames, because of the amazing varieties of straw boaters and bonnets they always clamped on their heads before venturing into water which at seven-thirty a.m. was so unruffled, so pellucid, that it seemed almost a vacancy, an absent element. The sea up to their necks, they would carry on the conversation they had started as they shuffled out of their dresses and into vast swimsuits, and, my own swim done, I would sit on what I hoped might be the isolation of a patch of wall I had chosen for myself, gazing towards the island of Angistri as it began to assemble its rocky, wooded outline from out of the morning mist. But then, their conversation-in-the-sea momentarily suspended, the Hattery would wade cumbrously ashore, take their towels from wherever they had draped them, and gather all about me, the conversation now resumed without let or hindrance. They rarely if ever greeted me, but they knew better than to leave me on my own. An Englishman, I might have thought they were being intrusive. They knew they were being hospitable.

Hospitality at Babi's stretched to include the various entertainers who during the course of an evening were allowed to wander among the tables, into whose pockets were stuffed drachm notes by the diners, and who, before they moved on to other tavernas, were invariably invited to drink a glass of restina and taste whatever food took their fancy. There was, for example, a semi-blind man with a wicked grin who brought with him a white-painted violin across which he scraped a bow while singing and whistling as though in accompaniment to some tune he was playing, although there was no tune because the violin was without strings. There was also a man of indeterminate age – he looked impossibly ancient but George said that he was no older than his own father – who failed to make forks and spoons disappear up the sleeves of the heavy overcoat he always wore, no matter what the temperature. Unlike Tommy Cooper, who after all really could do tricks, this man couldn't. Or if he could, he never did. The laughter and applause he got came from displays of incompetence so absolute that you felt they must be rehearsed. George disagreed.

'But he always fails to do exactly the same tricks,' I said.

'That's because there are no other tricks he can't do,' George said.

Blame it on the retsina.

You could also blame retsina, or something stronger, perhaps – ouzo? raki? – on the woefully inadequate performances of a singer-guitarist who would from time to time stumble into the taverna and perform for half an hour or so, seemingly indifferent to applause that was sympathetic rather than enthusiastic. I must on one occasion have betrayed my irritation at his far from skilful playing and at his cracked voice, at the thin, undifferentiated drizzle of words, because Dimitris explained that the man, down-at-heel, with grey hair that hung in greasy strands over his ears – unusual, given that Greek men usually took great pride in their hair – had once been a successful, much-sought-after performer, but that under the junta he had been persecuted for his left-wing opinions, had been on more than one occasion arrested and beaten up, that work had been hard to come by – 'nobody dared employ him' – and that he had perhaps not surprisingly found solace in the bottle.

'Some of these people who clap now,' George said, 'informed on him back then.'

'What, people sitting at these tables?'

'Sure.'

I looked around me at the crowded taverna. People were smiling, some with their hands high above their heads as they applauded the guitarist.

'So they clap to ease their guilty consciences.'

'Oh no,' George said. 'It is not so simple. They were one thing then. Now it is different. Most of these people will not have really been friends of the bastards, but they had to survive. It is something Greeks know how to do. We learnt under the Turks. We are good at it.' And he told me that in the late 1960s, as a national serviceman in Crete, he was sent for by the commanding officer of the camp where he was stationed. 'I was very much nervous, because, you know, he may have heard something I said that was disrespectful. There were informers everywhere and sometimes they would make up stories if they didn't like you or thought you were against the junta. Just to get you into trouble and earn themselves some praise. But thanks be to God, the general wanted to see me about another matter. You see, I spoke English and some French, so he asked me to work in the post room.'

'Really? Why?'

'As a censor, a spy. I was to open letters and inspect them for any bad remarks about the junta and tell the general if I found evidence for a plot against the colonels.'

'And what did you say?'

'I said yes. If I'd said no I'd have been arrested.'

'Not nice.'

George shrugged. He was taught, so he explained, to steam open letters and then re-seal them. 'Of course none of the soldiers wrote in French or English. They were poor country boys sending notes to their parents and sweethearts. Most of them could hardly write. "I am well, I hope you are. I love you." Sometimes I wrote their letters for them. They would pay me what they could – food, a bottle of wine. So I would open and read my own letters.' George paused, giggled, then said, 'there was a sergeant who had to overlook my work in the post room and he could hardly read. Sometimes, when I came across one of my own letters I would tell him that this was a particularly good one: you know, loyal. Then he would ask for the name of the soldier and the soldier might be rewarded.'

'How?'

'As we all were: with food. A bottle of wine.' George shook his head at the comic absurdity of it all. 'Anyway, everybody knew their letters were opened so nobody would risk saying anything dangerous in them. If you wanted to speak what was on your mind you waited until you were with friends you could trust' – here George thrust out his tongue and gripped it between thumb and forefinger before releasing it with a flourish – 'and *then* you talked.'

'So it was all a waste of time.'

'Oh, no.' George speared a morsel of lamb cutlet. 'I was taken off parade-ground duty and I was allowed to visit home more often, and besides sometimes there was some extra…' He made a large scooping gesture with his right hand before thrusting it into his trouser pocket.

I looked around. It being a Saturday night, Babi's was full to bursting, and among those who crowded round the tables to eat, drink and laugh with their families and friends, were some, so George insisted, who ten years previously would have been in the pay of the colonels and yet who were now rubbing shoulders with others the junta had harmed, including the broken down singer at present shuffling between tables, pausing at some to drink, at others to allow coins and notes to be pushed into his coat pockets, and shaking hands with all.

It was too much for me. 'Damned if I understand it,' I said. 'You're telling me that this poor man is shaking hands with people who did him damage, right in front of our noses. Why doesn't he hit them?'

And again George said, 'It is not that simple. You did what you could to help,' he added, to my mind mysteriously, although, when on a future occasion I heard someone else say the same thing, I began to understand something of the labyrinthine ways Greeks found to steer themselves and others to survival under Papadopoulos and his thugs.

Because Babi's was always so crowded on Saturdays, from time to time we'd try elsewhere. One place we briefly took to patronising was called The Taverna of the Three Brothers. It was rather more up-market than Babi's, with parquet flooring and wood-panelled walls rather than concrete and distemper, and the cutlery, made of steel, unlike Taverna ta Spata's cheap tin utensils, didn't bend. Most of our group claimed to like going to the place, although George and I were less enthusiastic, not so much because it was at least as crowded as Babi's but because whereas at Babi's people came to eat and drink and meet friends, here people came to see and be seen. The women typically wore fur coats over expensive dresses, the men had on tan or biscuit-coloured suits, and both men and women flashed gold at neck and wrist. Here, we were among but definitely not of the fashionable. We were not, therefore, among those who could expect any favours from the brothers. No fetching our own retsina, no friendly deliberation over dishes, and certainly no possibility of reserving a table.

This became a problem. We'd arrive at our usual time of ten o'clock, all the tables bar one would be taken, and we'd have to stand about, sometimes for the best part of an hour, before space could be found for us. 'Us' meant George, Elias, Dimitris and sometimes though not always his fiancée, Aleka, and Manos and Fotini. I suspect Manos in particular, anxious, solicitous, and entirely well-intentioned, felt that The Three Brothers was a more seemly place for a professor of English to be seen eating his Saturday meal at than Babi's, with its higgledy-piggledum, its charivari of sounds and smells, its joyous sense of carnival. But of course it was precisely that I loved, as I did not love the crowd who gathered here, drawn not by food and drink – inferior to anything Spata could offer – but by the lure of seeing the national basketball team, a bunch of well-muscled, tall and 'haughty athletes', who regularly dined at the taverna on Saturday nights because among them was the son of The Three Brothers.

The team ate for free but by doing so earned the taverna fame and, no doubt, a moderate fortune. At that time, basketball was a major sport in Greece, the national team one of the best in Europe; and their guaranteed presence at The Three Brothers was enough to draw many to the place. You knew when the team was about to make its entrance from a sudden tightening of the atmosphere. The customary raucous conversations would dwindle into whisperings, women took out compacts in order to adjust make-up, twiddled with their hair, resettled fur coats across their shoulders, and each time the door opened everyone craned or half-stood for a better view before falling disconsolately back if, as sometimes happened, the newcomer turned out to be a chance would-be diner. A quick shake of the head from one of the brothers and out into the night the luckless man would go.

And then, finally, the door would open wide, and slowly, in single file, came the gladiators. As one by one they entered the applause would start, growing from hesitant hand-claps to unabashed cheers as they marched the length of the taverna to the large table reserved for them, where the brothers waited to greet them, to shake hands, to have their cheeks kissed. People stood to watch, women flashed their eyes – 'me first, Kingsley' – and then, with the team finally seated, the taverna could return to its usual hubbub of sounds.

Beautiful, lofty things, those sportsmen, answering to some need for hero-worship that is deep in the Greek psyche, as in most. I thought of the time, some months previously, when I had been taken to the National Theatre for the opening night of *Heartbreak House*, directed – very badly as it proved – by Jules Dessin. A few minutes before curtain up, and with most of the audience in their seats, there was a sudden stir, followed by clapping that quickly swelled into a storm of applause. Two men stood framed in the entry to the stalls, one thick set, his fleshy face topped by a mass of dark, wavy hair, the other slight, frail, stooped, with a thin, gingery beard. Who were they? Theodorakis and Ritsos, my companion explained. Afterwards I was taken backstage and there got to shake Ritsos's hand. I too have my heroes.

Our visits to The Three Brothers went on for several more Saturdays, but always there was the irritation of having to wait for a table to become free before we could be seated, followed by the further irritation of slow and perfunctory service and frankly inferior food. One night, as we stood dully in line, I suggested that matters might be improved were we to arrive at the taverna half an hour earlier. My remark was greeted with cries of amazed approval. Of course, of course, that was what we must do. The next Saturday I arrived at The Three Brothers at the earlier time we had agreed. The rest arrived half an hour later. We had an unusually long wait for a table. After that, I insisted we went back to Babi's.

One mid-week evening George and I were there on our own when Babi came to our table, a smile on his lips and a sheep's skull in his hands. 'A special gift for you, Mr John.' He prised the skull apart and shook the contents onto my plate. I didn't greatly care for the look of the white mush but George at once got busy on it, and while he did so Babi produced from his apron pocket a scrap of paper which looked to have been torn from a newspaper and gave it me to read. 'FOR SALE. United Distilleries Scotland wish to dispose of four hundred barrels, formerly used for storing whisky.' That was the gist of it.

'Mr John,' Babi asked, 'where in Scotland is this United Distilleries?'

'Not a clue. Probably somewhere near the top, but I really don't know.'

'But you can find out?'

Yes, I said, I could find out. But why did he want to know?

'Because I want to buy these barrels.'

Babi? Buy four hundred whisky barrels? Why? What for? What *with*?

As though he could mind read, Babi reached down inside the top of his apron and produced the most enormous fistful of drachm notes. 'I have money,' he said, 'I go to this place, I buy these barrels, I make more money. You find me the address of this place, that is all I want.'

I did as he asked and forgot all about it.

The following week Babi was missing from the taverna for a few nights. 'Babi, he gone to Scotland,' was all one of the brothers told us.

But by the weekend he was back, and in expansive mood. 'Mr John, for you, something special.' And a large piece of Danish blue cheese was put before me. He then sat down with us, a thing he rarely did if, as now, the taverna was busy. A grin that, were it on anyone else's face I would have thought of as smug, widening his stubbly cheeks, he told us of how, the previous Monday, he had left Athens on the first morning flight for Heathrow, had from London boarded a commuter plane bound for Edinburgh, and had finished his journey by train and taxi, arriving at his destination early in the afternoon. 'So I see the barrels which I like very much and I argue a little about the price, you know, and then I buy them.'

Argue a little! Like all Greeks Babi was an habitual haggler and though I never found out how much he managed to have knocked off the asking price, it would have been enough to satisfy his pride and yet accomplished with such skill as to leave the other side feeling they'd got the better of the bargain. His journey to Scotland, he explained, had been plotted for him by 'a cousin' – of course – who worked for Olympic Airlines. 'And he has some cousins in Aberdeen. A nice town. So I stay there on Monday night then I come back to London where I stay with another cousin, a very nice lady, and I do some shopping, you know, and then I come home.'

Two questions occurred to me. In the first place, how had Babi paid for the barrels? Greeks seldom had large bank accounts and almost never wrote cheques. There were of course good reasons for this. In addition to distrusting the banking system – banks regularly went into liquidation or simply vanished into thin air, taking their clients' money with them – the Greek 'black' economy meant that nearly everyone dealt in ready cash, which couldn't be traced by the tax inspectors. 'Greece is a poor country full of rich people,' was how it was once put to me, and while I knew people who were genuinely poor and heard of others who were poorer still, it was certainly the case that nobody ever declared their full earnings. They didn't tell their friends and they didn't tell officialdom. And anyway, payment for services rendered was often in kind. A form of barter economy survived in the Greece I knew then. In Babi's, for example, you'd often find men, sometimes alone, more often with their families – electricians, plasterers – who had done work for the taverna and were being paid in kind – that is, by a week of free meals, or as many as were thought fit repayment for the work rendered. True, from time to time Babi would peel off some notes from the vast roll that swelled his apron front and press them into hands that weren't so much open and waiting as discreetly available. But I noticed that when he did this, neither he nor the man whom he was paying ever looked at each other. It was as though there was something slightly shameful about a cash transaction, something not quite honourable.

Babi probably kept that vast roll of drachm notes under his floorboards. But I couldn't see British businessmen accepting payment in 'fat and sweltering' drachms. Nor, as it turned out, had they. Babi had changed drachms to pounds before leaving Athens and, once the deal was concluded, handed over the due amount in crisp Bank of England notes. I never found out how much he had paid but it must have run well into the thousands. I thought of him travelling alone to the north of Scotland, his pockets stuffed with cash. Had he not been worried he might be jumped? But then I looked at his muscled arms, those massive shoulders. You'd have to be a brave or extremely foolish dip to take on Babi. Before I could put my second question, he left us to deal with other customers.

But several weeks later I got the answer. I was working in my flat one afternoon when the phone rang. 'Mr John, you are at home. Good. I want you to come with me, I have something to show you. In half an hour exactly I come to your flat. We are going to take a trip in my car. OK?'

'OK,' I said.

An hour later – 'I am not so late that it matters, you agree?' – we were making our way across Athens in Babi's old Cortina. He was in an unusually good mood, singing a succession of *rembetika* songs, banging on the steering-wheel with the flat of his hand, throwing his head from side to side, refusing to tell me where we were going or why. Then, brought by a route I had failed to recognise, I saw that we'd arrived at Piraeus.

Babi swung the car across the two-way traffic and drove, more slowly now, along the concrete concourse that ran the length of the immense waterfront. We passed ferries, large and small, a few being loaded up, more standing idle, for this was out of season; we passed smaller craft that regularly plied between Piraeus and Aegina, and which were on the water at all times of year, we passed what could have been a mine-sweeper, in urgent need of a fresh coat of paint to cover the streaks and splodges of rust showing through its gun-metal grey, we passed a clutch of fishing boats, and then, right at the end of the docks, we came to a small container ship.

Babi stopped the car. 'This is what we come to see,' he said, motioning me to get out. We walked towards the ship and as we came near, Babi called out, 'Nikos, *Nikos.*'

A man appeared in the prow of the ship. He was wearing a white-topped cap and dark-blue coat with brass buttons and gold-edged lapels. He shouted a greeting and waved to Babi, then pointed to two of the containers stacked high along the deck.

'My cousin,' Babi said, and his guttural voice was suddenly thick with emotion. 'He is a sea-captain. He bring the barrels for me.'

I've no idea how many barrels Babi kept for himself and how many he sold on, but both Dimitris and George were convinced that the trip to Scotland had resulted in a whacking great profit. Old whisky barrels were much prized by taverna owners, because the impregnated wood was, it seemed, perfect for giving an added flavour to even the finest retsina and also for ensuring it remained good to the last drop. No doubt about it, Babi had struck gold.

'Well, good for him,' I said. 'Many more deals like that and he can retire.'

They looked at me as though I were mad. *Retire*? the look meant, and what then would Babi *do*?

And Now the Women

And now a bird emerges from a cloud
flies over the rooftops and descends upon the town
time was it stayed locked in the moon for years
no wonder it's embittered glittering
and has one huge gleaming female eye

It cuts through rain clouds
floats like a ghost over rooftops
in the streets they call to it bird bird of rain
but it won't pause in its flight because if it did
thousands of fingers would reach for it
because it's tough smeared in blood
wild and falls on the town with the rain
and has the one huge gleaming female eye

That's why women thrill when they see it
some hide it in their mirrors
some in their wardrobes
others so deep in their bodies
the men who embrace them at night can't see it
nor in the morning as they rummage for clothes
nor as they dress before the mirror

Because this bird's very bitter very bright
very frightened

After the Greek of Miltiades Sachtouris

CHAPTER FIVE

The Mini-Skirt

O NE EVENING in late November '84 some American friends invited me to accompany them to a special showing of the film *The Killing Fields*. It proved to be an odd, even bizarre occasion. In the first place the showing was at the American College, a lavishly funded school in one of the Athenian suburbs. I was used to seeing films in various clamorous flea-pits scattered the length and breadth of the city, places wild with noise, chokingly-thick smoke, and uninhibited audience participation, where celluloid villains were hissed, heroes as routinely applauded, and heroines invited to step out of the screen for the sexual opportunity of a lifetime. Sophisticated it wasn't, but going to the cinema always cheered me up, even though the projection was invariably poor and on occasions downright execrable, and notwithstanding the fact that the film was always stopped exactly halfway through and regardless of what was happening on-screen: we could be in the middle of a subtle interchange between two important characters, say, or a car chase, or a passionate love encounter, when up would come the lights. Time for an ice cream or a drink.

Nothing like that at the American College. The auditorium was carpeted in sage-green, the same suavely expensive material covered the walls and the deep-sprung tip-up seats, and while the film was watched in smoke-free silence, there was beforehand a lavish reception. Cocktails, canapés, women in little black numbers with pearl necklaces, dark-suited men, handshakes, rows of gleaming teeth exchanging the same polite, meaningless talk. 'Hi, I'm Bob, and this is my wife, Ellen. Ellen, I want you to meet John. He's a Professor at the University. Guess that's a job and a half.' And then, before I could speak, the words and grin were re-directed. 'Hi, I'm Bob, this is my wife, Ellen. Ellen, I want you to meet...' And the next invitee would be passed down the line to a waiting tray.

Who was Bob? I never found out. Someone in the American Embassy, I suppose, perhaps connected to the Cultural Attaché. Holding a glass of whisky – 'Can I freshen that for you, sir' – I looked about me at those tanned, serious men and their wives and partners, the women's immaculate coiffures, their discreetly expensive jewellery, their voices pitched at a level just above intimacy. I tried to imagine any of them at Babi's, then gave it up as a sudden ripple of attention indicated the arrival of An Important Person. And there, suddenly, striding into the circle that formed to greet her was Melina Mercouri, Minister of Culture and Greece's unofficial First Lady. Though she was already thin from the lung cancer that would eventually kill her, her gaunt beauty, vivid green, full-length dress, and the gold accoutrements that lit up every part of her person gave her a glamour that seemed a world away from the held rectitude of the others. She was out of place, surely, and not just because of her flamboyance. After all, she had been second to none in denouncing the presence of American air force bases in Athens and, by extension – which sometimes became outright excoriation – American policy in the Mediterranean. Not even Papandreou could outdo her in this. It was at least partly because of Melina that my students so regularly marched in protest to the American Embassy, that they stoned windows of the American Hilton, burnt the Stars and Stripes. So what was she doing here?

Being a film star, was the answer. Her entry had clearly been timed for maximum effect. She was late, but who cared? Stars are allowed a delayed entrance. And as the men and women gathered round her, eager to shake her hand and, for some, be richly rewarded by air kisses, and as they watched her take a cigarette from the packet she carried in one hand – Marlboro I noticed before the fingers with their encrusting rings and deep-red nails closed round it – and as she put the cigarette to her carmined lips and waited for someone to step forward with a light (there was no question of her lighting her own cigarette, any more than there was of her obeying the prominently displayed 'No Smoking' signs) – as all this happened I wondered whether anyone else was thinking that her attendance at this event and the behaviour of her hosts was, well, just a bit hypocritical, wasn't it?

Call it diplomacy.

Anyway, now that she was here, it was time for the film to begin. As the lights dimmed, we settled into our seats.

Afterwards, the audience – which, with the exception of Melina, her entourage and a few invited guests like myself, seemed entirely composed of Americans – regrouped, and I was struck by the fact that people, if they spoke at all, did so in whispers. But for the most part they nodded farewells, raising a hand in silent salutations of departure. Only when we had got back into the car that had brought us to the College did either of my hosts, the American professor at Athens University and his funny, friendly wife, speak. 'Jesus,' he said, 'what's the world going to think of us?'

'Not badly enough,' I thought of saying, but didn't. It would have been smug, and besides, he was in shock, as I now realised that most of the audience must have been. It wasn't that they were ignorant of what Kissinger had done when he extricated America from the Vietnam war. I'd had several opportunities to talk to Americans in Athens, and I didn't find one who was in any way sympathetic to the Nixon-Kissinger covert arrangement by which Cambodia had been abandoned to Pol Pot's murderous regime. But knowing and seeing were different matters. Because in the film you were forced to witness murder on a mass scale, were required to understand exactly how it was licensed by official American lies and the furtive cut-and-run evasion of responsibility towards people who had every reason to believe America would protect them. The film left no place to hide from the truth that American policy had led directly to the killing fields. And now that it was about to be shown world-wide, everyone would share in that truth. Hatred of America, loathing and contempt for its governmental deviousness, its failure of responsibility to the weak and the lame, would be spread across the globe. And even more than that, I suspect, my friends were in deep shock at the revelation that *they* couldn't any longer uphold a belief in American goodness.

'Not badly enough.' I had wanted to protest that the camera lingered too long and too often on the face of the American reporter in Cambodia at the time of the evacuation, registering *his* anguish, *his* sense of betrayal. This was Hollywood doing its damnedest to soften the film's meaning. America may have behaved badly, but it's nevertheless an *American* who knows this and, more tellingly, who *feels* it, who is therefore the film's moral centre. The sufferings of the Cambodians are displaced, by no means glossed over, but not given anything like the degree of attention that's paid to one American, who here wears the reporter's badge of courage that in an earlier film would have been the sheriff's tin star. Something wrong there, surely? But my view was that of an outsider, and being English and growing up at a time of post-colonial disillusionment about claims of empire, I couldn't share my friends' belief in those American values they took for granted as being good for the world and therefore endlessly exportable.

In silence we drove to the house of a Greek friend, a woman academic, who had invited us back for drinks.

But inside her well-appointed flat, high above the city, there was a buzz of talk, even an occasional laugh. I chatted with a younger woman, also an academic, one of the few members of staff who'd bothered to introduce themselves to me when I'd begun my teaching duties, and with whom I'd from time to time enjoyed an early evening drink at one of the bars that ringed the building where we both had our offices. Although I wasn't convinced Christina knew as much about literature as she claimed – 'who is that man?' she had once loudly and imperiously demanded, while pointing at a photograph of T S Eliot on the front of a book I was carrying – she was amusing company, especially when describing her current lover's fits of jealous behaviour, which she would recount in considerable detail. 'Every time he comes to my flat he begins by lifting the lavatory seat. He wants to see whether another man has been here and made pee-pee. Can you imagine.' Knowing that I was expected to say that I could – and in truth she was a very attractive woman, slender, well-proportioned, with a smooth, olive complexion, generous mouth and huge, coal-black eyes – I nodded with what I hoped was enigmatic sympathy.

That revelation had been made, full-throttle, in a bar near Syntagma Square where, although it was off my usual beat, I once or twice agreed to meet students, and where, on the occasion she came with us, it turned out that she knew many of the clientele, mostly older men. 'Politicians,' one of the students later told me. 'Her father is a leading member of New Democracy. He was a general at the time of the junta.' They didn't like her, intimated that she owed her academic post to her father's influence.

Very probably she did, but then from what I'd heard just about everyone in the department owed his or her appointment to people known, favours called in, promises made good. And not all were as lively company. I wondered what she had made of the film we'd just seen.

She countered my question with one of her own. 'Did you like it?'

Not especially, I was going to say, but then, I don't know why, instead told her that there was one scene I hadn't understood. 'It's when the Cambodian our hero is to befriend has been captured by the Khmer Rouge. You remember? He and others who've been rounded up are shown grouped under a tree, waiting to be shot. A man comes to him, one of Pol Pot's, sees the badge or whatever it is he has hanging round his neck, then drags him into the sun and leaves him there without food or water all day. By the end of the day he's nearly dead of dehydration, but he survives. Now, why wasn't he just shot along with the rest?'

'Because the man was trying to save him.'

'Really?'

'Yes, really. That badge round his neck, it had been taken from a car, a Mercedes Benz, I think, and all the boys in a gang would wear one. It was a sign of membership. The man who had orders to kill him saw the badge and so instead tried to save his life.'

'Seems a funny way to do it, leaving him in the sun all day without any water.'

She looked at me, and her look was a mixture of scorn and incredulity. 'He had to be careful. If he'd made it obvious he was helping a friend, he himself would have been killed. Don't you understand?'

And all at once I did. Understood, too, that as someone who had lived through the junta she had inevitably learnt strategies for survival. 'Sorry for being so dumb,' I said, and meant it.

She accepted my apology with a brief smile. 'You do what you can to help,' she said.

She left not long after that, and soon enough the party thinned out to a few stragglers. I was about to say my own farewells when my hostess asked me to stay behind. 'There is something I want to speak to you about.'

She saw others to the door, then rejoined me in the now empty room where the drinks had been served and where, having carried the many full-to-overflowing ashtrays into the kitchen and emptied them into a bin, I was beginning to pile glasses onto a large tray I'd brought from the kitchen while she stood in the hall to say her prolonged goodnights to various friends and colleagues.

'Leave that,' she said peremptorily. Then, lighting a cigarette, 'Would you like another drink? Whisky, perhaps? Johnnie Walker? Cutty Sark?' For some reason, Cutty Sark was the Athenians' favourite scotch.

'A beer would be ideal.'

'In the fridge,' she said, motioning to the kitchen, 'and bring me an ashtray, will you, please.' Her manner was oddly formal, not exactly unfriendly, but in no sense warm. Puzzled as to what she had in mind to say to me – some unwelcome home truth? Some revelation about the department? Some legal matter for which she might be seeking my advice? – I took beer and ashtray back to where she now sat relaxedly on a long, white leather sofa, one arm draped over its back, legs drawn up under her. She took the ashtray from me and, without speaking, motioned me to a chair opposite.

Only when I had sat and taken a first sip of beer did she speak.

'About Christina,' she said, looking directly at me.

What about Christina? She surely didn't think I'd been flirting with her, did she? Was she going to warn me against the jealous boyfriend? If so, she had no need. Quite apart from the fact that I was a happily married man, Christina wasn't my type. I wasn't even sure whose type – save the boyfriend's – she could be. She reminded me of Henry James's description of Henrietta Stackpole: friendly, undeniably attractive, but somehow shining and 'obvious'.

'You know she's not popular with the students?'

'I had heard something to that effect, yes.'

She laughed. 'You English,' she said. Then, 'And no doubt you know why. Her father worked for the junta and she has her post because her father still has influence with government officials. That is what they say.'

'Is it true?'

When she didn't reply, I said, 'And university posts depend on official – government – approval. I have to say I don't understand that. Or rather, now you've a socialist government, why should people who were sympathetic to the junta have any say in what goes on? Why aren't they in prison, if it comes to that?'

'Because there aren't enough prisons to hold them all,' she said, as though explaining matters to an unusually slow child. Her look suggested that she was weighing the advisability of some revelation. When she spoke again, it was more slowly, deliberately. 'Besides, you have to distinguish between those who behaved badly and those who just got on with running the country, or minding their business, or coping as well as they could in the circumstances. And even if Christina's father was not a nice man, that is no reason to attack his daughter.'

'I've never heard that the students make life difficult for Christina.'

She drew deeply on her cigarette before she replied. 'I don't think they have – yet. But they might. The second-year students in particular are a very politicised group.' She paused. 'As you know,' she said.

Ah. I thought I saw where this was leading. I was friendly with some of the student leaders, therefore I could be useful in calling them off should they take it into their heads to go on the attack against Christina, demand her resignation, make life unbearable for her.

'You know she hasn't a doctorate?'

'I didn't.'

'And without a doctorate you're not supposed to be given a permanent contract.'

'What Americans call "tenure"?'

'Exactly.'

'And Christina has got tenure?'

She nodded, and looked at me, a look whose meaning I couldn't read. Was I expected to say more?

I said, 'I'm pretty sure the students I talk to don't care about such matters. What they care about is being responsibly taught, which to be honest they often aren't, are they? Though I've never heard them complain of Christina in that regard. Nor you, of course,' I added, meaning it.

Perhaps she doubted my sincerity, because, with the slightest of smiles, she said, 'Ever the diplomat.'

That stung me. I said, 'I was telling the truth.' When she said nothing, I added, 'But let me ask you a question.' Still she said nothing, merely looked at me. I said, 'Why do you care about Christina? From what you say she's done well enough for herself. But you? Weren't you badly treated under the junta?'

Again the nod, the level gaze, the silence. She played with one of the rings on her fingers, then finally said, 'What have you heard about that?'

'Only that you lost your lectureship, were dismissed from the university. Isn't that so?' Someone, perhaps Manos but I couldn't recall, had one evening run through a list of names of academics whom the junta had removed from their university posts. During the years following 1968 students became used to enrolling for courses under Lecturer A that would suddenly and without prior announcement be placed under the stewardship of Lecturer B. What had happened to A? You learnt not to ask. Afterwards, with the junta ringleaders in prison and democracy restored, some of the dismissed academics came back from internal exile, others were released from jail, still others returned from years spent abroad. Not all, however. Some of those who had found work in overseas universities preferred to stay where they were. A few were never heard of again. All I knew for certain of my hostess was that she had been a young lecturer at the university when Papadopoulos and his gang were shoehorned into power, and that soon after their arrival she lost her university post. Now she was once more working at the university, an admired academic with an important book on modern Greek literature to her name. But the junta had cost her seven years of her life. Why should she be so exercised about the fate of one of its erstwhile supporters?

'I will tell you what happened,' she said, as though reading my mind. 'Maybe then you will understand.' A pause while another cigarette was lit. I took a pull on my beer and waited. 'When the junta came in I had been teaching at the university for two years. I was very happy. I was doing what I had yearned to do, research, write, and teach good students. Christina was one of those students. Then,' – she made a downward chopping motion with both her hands – 'these bloody bastards arrive, and I am in trouble. One day, I am called to the Ministry of Education. I am told I have lost my job. I am a danger to the morals of my students. You know why?'

'I can't imagine.'

'Because I wear a mini-skirt.' Her laugh was deep, derisive. 'A mini-skirt, you see, is a sign of decadence. It will inflame the passion of my boy students and give a bad example to the girl students. So I must pack my bags and go.'

'Laughable if it hadn't been so disgusting,' I said. 'Had any of the students complained?' Christina, I was thinking.

'I doubt it, although you could never be sure. There were those who were friends to your face and enemies behind your back. Who could you trust? Very few. But of course the mini-skirt was an excuse. I was the author of some articles and shorter pieces that had appeared in socialist journals and newspapers. That was why they wanted me out. And the clothes I wore indicated that I did not accept the traditional role for women in our society and that, too, was a danger. Altogether, I was a bad lot.'

'So what happened?'

'I was dismissed from the university and of course I could find no other work. Journalism was out of the question because all the left-wing papers had been shut down and I was *persona non grata* among the rest. And then I was threatened with prison because I printed my own satiric account of my dismissal and tried to distribute it among friends. Somehow it got into the hands of those for whom it was certainly not intended. So. The knock on the door. Into a police wagon, court, and an order to reappear for sentencing the following week.' Another pause, another cigarette.

'And?' I asked.

Again the deep laugh. 'I never went back. By the time they came looking for me I was out of the country, in London can you believe, and with some teaching work at a London training college.'

I drank the last of my beer, saw her amused, challenging gaze directed at me, and said, 'You're going to tell me that Christina arranged your escape.'

'Correct. Or to speak more accurately, Christina didn't arrange it herself, but she talked to her father and *he* arranged it.' How exactly, she never knew. But the evening after her court appearance there was another knock at the door and, waiting outside, she found a young man who handed her a note from Christina, asking her to accompany him to her, Christina's, house. Although she suspected a trick, she decided to go with him. The house, in one of Athens's classier suburbs, had a military policeman on guard who let them through after the man accompanying her had flashed a pass, and a maid in black dress and white, frilly apron ushered them into a large, ground-floor room where Christina sat with yet another man, this one balding, wearing a heavy, dark-blue suit, a briefcase propped at his feet. Without saying a word to her, with only the briefest of unsmiling eye contact, Christina got up and left the room. She was motioned to a chair, and the man in the suit explained that it had been decided – by whom, she was not told – that for her own safety she would be leaving Greece and that employment had been arranged for her in London. As he said this, he drew from the briefcase some papers and handed them to her. They included a passport, letters of introduction, and, in a large brown envelope, a number of brand-new English banknotes. Almost before she could absorb this extraordinary piece of information, she heard him tell her that as soon as the interview was over she would be escorted home by the man who had brought her, she would then pack no more than two suitcases of clothes, books and papers, would not be allowed to contact anyone – in fact, he told her, her telephone had already been disconnected – and she would then be taken to the airport and put on a plane for Heathrow.

When he finished speaking, she sat trying to take in all he had said. After a few minutes' silence he asked her whether she had any *reasonable* questions to put to him, and the way he stressed the word reasonable made plain that whatever she wanted to know would certainly be withheld. Above all, who was responsible for this plan to get her out of Greece. But one question had to be asked. Couldn't she at least tell her parents what was happening to her? Yes, she would be permitted to phone them from the airport. That was his one concession. And supposing she refused the offer, if offer it was? Suppose she decided to stay, to turn up at court, to argue her case? Then, she was told, she would go to prison, and he did not propose to spell out the consequences of *that*. Nor did he need to. She knew, they all knew, of the atrocities that went on in the various prisons, on the mainland and even more on the islands. Torture, rape, starvation, 'suicide'. She did as he directed.

And seven years later, after the restoration of democracy, she returned to Athens with an English husband, since abandoned, a daughter, and the promise that her university post would be returned to her.

After she'd finished her tale we sat silent, my eyes directed out of the window towards the lights of the city below, her gaze, I could tell, on me. Eventually, I said, 'Do you ever talk to Christina about... about that period?'

Her laugh was dismissive. 'Of course not.'

'What? Not at all?'

'Not at all. Far better to keep quiet. We know what we need to know.'

'And that includes the fact that she helped you then and you therefore want to help her now.'

'I want to make sure she is not unjustly treated by people who do *not* know about the past, that is all. And now we will change the subject.'

I left soon after that, steered my way downhill to the thoroughfare above which she lived. It was crammed with late-night revellers at a street party that had been organised, so banners proclaimed, by the Euro-Communists. What would *they* make of the story I'd just heard? Then it occurred to me that there must be many such stories from the years of the junta and, for that matter, ones that went back through Greece's history. Persians, Romans, Venetians, Turks, Germans, to say nothing of home-grown dictators such as Metaxas, Papadopoulos, Ionnides and their henchmen. All had to be outwitted, or prevented from doing their worst: against all of them you learnt how to do what you could to help others. Silence, exile and cunning weren't just for Leninists.

End of Day

When we meet you don't know yourself.
You lean to a mirror
and see ancient faces: so
Homer's people emerge
mouths agape, thirsty from their dark world.
Can you be sure you know them?
They want snapshots for company,
they need food, newspapers, the radio.
They fill the house. They're hanging out of windows,
they block the street, they're all over town.
Everything stops. What time is it?
Water dries up. And now we're thirsty, too,
we who are outside, and then the panic starts:
Sirens, flashing lights, barricades.

(In yourself
there's scarcely breathing space:
certainly no room for you.)

Cars, trucks, crammed with people
all heading for the mountains.
The talk's of lifeless verbs,
of rhymes laid out in the morgue.
Our town is emptied now.
Only, a breathless horse
bolts from your eyes, steaming.

From the Greek of Yannis Kontos

CHAPTER SIX

Meeting Poets

ARLY IN THE NEW YEAR of 1985 Andrew Motion, who was
at that time editor of *Poetry Review*, suggested I might like
to write a piece for the journal about the state of
contemporary Greek poetry. I wrote back to say that the idea
interested me but that I'd want to enlist the help of the poet and
dramatist Andreas Angelakis, whom I'd met a few months earlier
and with whom I'd struck up a friendship. Andreas, I pointed out,
inevitably knew far more about the subject than I did. My
proposal was fine by Andrew, and so Andreas and I set to work.
Our piece, the product of several bibulous meetings at a taverna
in the Plaka which Andreas liked partly because of the deserved
renown of its *stiffado* and partly because at an earlier period it had
been a favourite with Seferis and other Greek writers, appeared in
the April issue, although by then Mick Imlah had taken over as the
journal's editor.

Good friends though we became, Andreas wasn't the first
Greek poet I met in Athens. Not long after my arrival, I arranged
to see Constantine Trypanis in his room at the Greek Academy,
one of three handsome neoclassical buildings near the city centre.
(The others are the Greek National Library and, in the middle, the
old university, which by the time I arrived housed the
Administration. Now there's a surprise.) Trypanis had served as
Minister of Culture in the first post-junta government, having
returned to his native land after years spent as Professor of
Byzantine Studies at Oxford, where it was rumoured he had so
few students that he was virtually free to devote himself to
compiling the *Penguin Book of Greek Verse* and to working on his
own poetry.

It was this that had led to our first meeting. In the autumn of 1957, when I was a second-year student at Reading University, I went round to John Wain's flat on the outskirts of town. I was there to interview him for the student magazine, *Tamesis*. John had by then ceased to be a lecturer in Reading's English department, but he still lived in Reading, held regular court in a local pub, The Brunswick Arms, and remained on friendly terms with some at least of his former colleagues. I wanted to ask him about his various roles as poet, critic and novelist, but serious progress was made difficult not merely by the extraordinary fez John chose to clamp onto his head, the tassel of which, as it fell across his eyes, he would swat grandly away, but by interruptions from a tall, distinguished-looking, swarthy-complexioned man in a grey suit – I could hear the *clack-clacking* of his typewriter in the adjoining room – who, without so much as a by-your-leave, insisted on reading out a poem he had obviously just torn from the machine. John would comment, more or less favourably, and the man would sweep out of the room. More *clack-clacking*. Then back he'd come. John eventually made the introductions – 'Trypanis, Lucas' – and we shook hands. I don't recall what, if anything, we found to say to each other, but I do recall thinking that Trypanis seemed far too large for John's poky flat.

He also seemed too large for the café where I next came across him, Fuller's Tea Rooms in Oxford. On this occasion I was with Ian Fletcher, poet, bookman, and John's replacement in Reading's English department. Ian had been summoned to see 'Costa', as he called Trypanis, because 'Costa' was having difficulties with some of the poems that would form part of his third Faber collection, *Pompeian Dog* (1964). (The previous ones were *The Stones of Troy* and *The Cocks of Hades*.) He had sent Ian the manuscript and now wanted Ian's comments. Trypanis began by ordering tea for us all – fair enough in the circumstances, although I can affirm that of all the writers I have ever known Ian remains champion of champions among those whose round never came up – before studying Ian's many emendations and suggestions. Each was initially rejected and by the end of our meeting all had been accepted. Looking through that collection now I am pretty sure I can guess aright the words and phrases Ian supplied, and they will invariably be the ones to lift a poem at least momentarily out of unredeemable drabness.

How did such undistinguished work find so distinguished a publisher? And how on earth did *Pompeian Dog* become a Poetry Book Society Choice? Trypanis certainly knew how to choose his friends. Did Seferis, I wonder, put in a word for him at Faber? Seferis was a friend of T S Eliot, Faber's poetry editor, and Trypanis's poems are in debt to the great Greek poet in subject-matter – both poets are almost obsessively concerned with reading the meaning of Greece, its history, its 'soul', through its landscape – and occasional stylistic mannerisms. Besides, Trypanis's English – as far as I know he wrote no poetry in his native language – is what a sympathetic commentator might call 'lofty', as Seferis can sometimes be. Yet where Seferis's loftiness has real grandeur, Trypanis's rhetorical over-reach gives his poems the air of being 'correct' translations from the original. As I suppose in a way they are. He may have written in English but I am certain that he thought in Greek.

Still, *pace* Christopher Ricks, Trypanis got at least one thing right. When *Pompeian Dog* appeared, Ricks reviewed it none too kindly in the *New Statesman*. He took particular exception to the second stanza of 'December Twenty Four': 'And the shed's floor sourly iced,/ Clings to the hooves of the cattle./ The legs of dim-eyed sheep rattle –/ A hard birth for Christ' ['Sourly' – that will be Ian]. Ricks was genially contemptuous of what he saw as the desperate rhyme word 'rattle', and at the time I was inclined to agree with him. But I was wrong. Since then I have climbed hillsides in the clear, bone-dry Aegean air as sheep scamper away at my approach; and believe me, the sound their legs make as they knock together is very like sticks being scraped against a length of railing. They rattle all right. Trouble is, the rhyme undoubtedly feels awkward, even maladroit.

Trypanis's admiration for Seferis was equalled by his enthusiasm for Cavafy, several of whose key poems he included in his Penguin anthology when it appeared in 1971. Among them are 'The God Abandons Antony', 'Ithaca', 'The City' and, of course, 'Waiting for the Barbarians', poems that have leapt all linguistic and cultural barriers to become the possession of Western civilisation as a whole. Seferis was however a different matter. I had difficulties with him, whether in Rex Warner's versions or the later, much-lauded translations made by Edmund Keeley and Philip Sherard. Then, praise be, not long after I had got to Athens, I came across Kimon Friar's anthology of *Modern Greek Poetry*, and read his translation of Seferis's 'The King of Asine'.

Like so many of Seferis's poems, 'The King of Asine' is a meditation on Greek history. It puts down taproots, as it were, to try to locate ways in which the past can be sensed as a living quality in modern Greece, survives as what Yeats would have called 'a presence'. It is not merely in poems that Seferis plumbs this issue. Essays of his, gathered together in English as *On the Greek Style*, are similarly preoccupied with what he calls in his essay on Makryannis

> the spiritual wealth of [the] race, handed on through the ages from millennium to millennium, from generation to generation, from the sensitive to the sensitive; persecuted and always alive, ignored and always present – the common lot of the Greek popular tradition.

The subject of this particular essay was one of the leaders of the Greek War of Independence, an 'unlettered' general who left behind the story of his life in the pages of which, as in the untaught art of Theophilus, Seferis finds the 'Greekness' that is true 'spiritual wealth'. As for 'The King of Asine', the trigger for this particular poem is a mysterious reference in the list Homer provides in the *Iliad* of those who sent arms and ships to Troy. 'Asine also', Homer says. And that is all. We are told nothing about the number of ships the king sent, nor of what happened to them and the men who sailed in them. Seferis's poem begins with him visiting the city's ancient site.

All that now remains of Asine is one tip of a wide bay, about ten miles south of Nafplion, and when with Manos and Fotini I went there for the first time in the spring of 1985 what looked like an abortive archaeological dig had been abandoned and the place, which we reached by walking through a succession of lemon and orange groves, seemed forlorn in its loneliness: a rocky hill with caves that might, I suppose, have once been burial chambers and, at the hill's base, trenches scored in the sandy soil. It must have looked very much the same when Seferis visited some time in the 1930s. Now Asine boasts a beach taverna; and at the opposite end of the bay, Tolon, a town with a growing number of disco-bars and hotels, fronts the Saronic gulf into whose blue waters the King of Asine's ships were launched.

Towards the end of his poem, Seferis the visitor

> looks at the stones and lingers, asking himself
> are there I wonder
> among these broken lines peaks edges hollows and curves
> are there I wonder …
> …the movement of feature the form of the affection
> of those who have so strangely dwindled in our lives…
> or no, perhaps nothing remains but the weight only
> nostalgia for the weight of a living existence

And the poem itself seems to be dwindling away, fading out in a trail of wispy speculation.

But then,

> The shield-bearing sun rose fighting
> and from the depths of a cavern a frightened bat
> crashed on the light, like an arrow on a shield:
> 'Asinin te…' 'Asinin te…' Was this the King of Asine
> for whom we have sought so carefully on this acropolis
> feeling at times with our fingers his touch upon the
>   stones.

You know where you were when you heard news of Kennedy's assassination? I know where I was when I first read that poem. Sitting in a little taverna off Acharnon Street, in early October, 1984. It was the meeting with that poem, in Friar's translation, that convinced me of Seferis's greatness and made me hungry for more. Slowly, I began to teach myself some Greek, and coincidentally, often guided by Manos and later Andreas, was introduced to the work of poets who had clearly learnt much from Seferis. Among them was one I found especially appealing, Takis Sinopoulos. My guess is that Sinopoulos is not much esteemed by Greek poets nowadays, but I admired what I read sufficiently to try to make my own English versions, greatly helped by Manos's expert guidance. And as I worked on the poems, so I found out all I could about the life of their author.

Sinopoulos was born in 1917. He trained as a doctor but with the outbreak of war in 1939, and following the abortive Italian invasion of Greece through Albania, he was conscripted into the army in which he seems to have fought against the Germans with great courage. Then, with peace, came the cynical carve-up of Europe. Greece had to be saved from communism. Those who had fought against fascism now became the internal enemy, and those who had collaborated or simply got away from Greece took power. (The version of this period presented in *Captain Corelli's Mandolin* has about as much basis in fact as Dr Moreau's island.) There followed the terrible civil war, which pitted family against family and did perhaps more damage than the Germans, for all their appalling brutality, had ever managed. I remember a television programme in which three old Greek women from a village somewhere in northern Greece talked about their memories of that time. One told of how her son, a republican, had been shot and killed by soldiers from a nearby village, his body left in no-man's land, where she could see it but was powerless to bring it in for burial. Eventually, a major from the other side came to collect it. He was unarmed and the women fell on him. 'What did you do?' one of them was asked.

'Tore him to pieces,' she said.

The Furies, I thought, looking at that lined face.

During the civil war Sinopoulos was recruited as an army officer and sent to serve in units in Thessaly and Macedonia. He was finally demobilised in 1949 and returned to his profession of medicine. At regular intervals from then until his death, he produced collections of poetry. An indebtedness to Seferis isn't in doubt, but to my ear, at least, Sinopoulos sounds his own note of plangent dignity in the face of disaster. 'Wherever I move Greece wounds me', Seferis famously wrote in his poem 'In the Manner of G S', composed just after the Metaxas dictatorship came to power in 1936, and many of Sinopoulos's poems are about the self-inflicted wounds of Greece.

This is true, above all, of 'Deathfeast', with its evocation of the Second World War and then, more horrifyingly, the civil war years, a time in which what Sinopoulos calls 'a black infection covered the map, Greece gasping for breath'. Yet the poem, which is among other things a long lament for the dead – Sinopoulos provides a litany of names – ends with a calming, restorative vision: of the fading away of old rivalries, of reconciled enemies, of a laying to final rest of antagonists who had remorselessly fed each other to the soil, whose pitiless heroism had caused such ravage. *C'est magnifique et c'est la guerre*. Anyway, it is civil war, that most 'terrible beauty'.

And writing down those words of Yeats it occurs to me how many similarities there are between the recent histories of Greece and Ireland. And how similar, too, their cultural resources. Both nations suffered under nearby, brutal oppressors, the freedom achieved by and for both remains partial and has been marked (and marred) by periods of civil war; and the terrible beauty of heroic sacrifice – the pursuit of integrity's grail – has been for both a mixed blessing. And this has been repeatedly testified to, explored and mourned over by a succession of great poets that each nation has produced, and who have sprung up in numbers out of all proportion, or so it may seem, to the total size of their populations.

Greece and Ireland are alike in other ways, too. Until very recently both were largely peasant societies under the domination of a church that was coercive and yet took care to preserve a deep cultural life (hedge schools, klephtic ballads), both value talk and hospitality above most other things – the empty chair by the hearth kept for the traveller – and in both the miraculous is swallowed as easily and naturally as daily bread. I think I can understand why in the 1920s the great Marxist classicist, George Thomson, decided that the European language into which he could most fittingly translate Aeschylus was Gaelic, for which reason he set himself to learn it.

Thomson's imagination was habituated to conflict and tragedy. I can imagine Sinopoulos bowing the knee in gratitude to Joyce's remark that 'history is a nightmare from which I am trying to awake.' The closing lines of 'Deathfeast' imagine an end to conflict, a closing of wounds:

> For the last time I gazed after them, called to them.
> The fire wasted to ash and through the window I saw
> how with just one star the night turns navigable
>
> how in an empty church the nameless dead
> are lain among heaped flowers, are anointed.

But history of a brutal kind returned once more with the CIA-backed junta of 1967. I was in America at the time and have a vivid memory of Dean Rusk, then LBJ's right-hand man as Secretary of State, tell his television audience that Greece was not yet ready for democracy, a remark so ineffable as to be beyond comment. It's a measure of the regard with which poetry is or at all events was held in Greece, that the colonels hoped Seferis would give the odour of legitimacy to their cause. To their chagrin and his eternal honour, he did no such thing, even refusing to publish any work while they remained in power. They were still wounding Greece when he died in 1971, leaving behind him a savage poem called 'The Aspalathoi', written shortly before his death, in which, at Sounion for the spring Feast of the Annunciation, he finds himself recalling a moment from Plato's *Republic*, which tells of the death of the tyrant Ardiaios, and of how his killers, having flayed him and drawn his body across the thorny *aspalathoi*, 'threw him into Tartarus, torn to shreds'. In this way, the poem ends,

> Ardiaios, the terrible Pamphylian tyrant,
> paid for his crimes in the nether world.

Springtime, the Feast to celebrate new life, and Sounion, where Byron, hero of Greek liberation, had carved his name. The properties are skilfully arranged to symbolise the inevitability of the colonels' downfall.

When the downfall came, it brought with it the freeing of thousands, including Yannis Ritsos, who as on previous occasions had been sent into internal exile and brutally ill-treated while he was there. Photographs of him as a young man, some taken before he had left his hometown of Monamvasia, show that he was always slight, even frail. The island prisons where he was sent and routinely abused, both physically and verbally, undoubtedly undermined his always precarious health. Not that this was likely to worry the colonels. Whereas Seferis, who had been awarded the Nobel Prize in 1963, was too famous for them to touch, Ritsos was in a very different, and far more vulnerable, position. He was after all a communist. When in 1977 he became a recipient of the Order of Lenin, there was no need for the colonels to lose any sleep over wondering whether the Western powers would intercede on Ritsos's behalf. He did not look for help, and no help came.

Ritsos was anyway used to official persecution. With Byron, that hero to Greeks, he could have said, 'I was born for opposition.' One of the first acts of the Metaxas dictatorship, when it seized power in 1936, was to organise the burning in public of Ritsos's 'Epitaphios'. This elegy had been composed after Ritsos saw the newspaper photograph of a mother kneeling beside the body of her son, a young tobacco-worker gunned down while taking part in a strike in Thessalonika earlier that year. The poem would later be set to music by Theodorakis, and in its musical form is now something of a modern classic as, for that matter, are many other famous Greek poems the same composer set. Or perhaps it would be more accurate to say that the poems became famous in and because of their musical versions. After the colonels were rounded up and locked away, Theodorakis's concerts regularly featured his settings of Ritsos, Seferis, Sikilianos and Elytis among others; and as a result, thousands of Greeks came to know by heart poems by the nation's great modern poets. I have been told that the famous uprising of November 17th, 1973, when students took to the streets of Athens around the Polytechnic, was triggered by a woman singer – one of the colonels' 'trusties' who deliberately betrayed their trust – introducing a line from Seferis into a song she sang on state TV. The line was 'Wherever I move Greece wounds me.' Though the uprising was put down with appalling ferocity – it is said that to this day nobody knows how many were killed, some of them

crushed to death under the tracks of American-supplied tanks – the students' action signalled the beginning of the end for the junta.

For all I know, the story about the singer may be apocryphal. What is beyond doubt is that until very recently Greek poets were venerated by their countrymen and women. Ritsos in particular became a hero to the young. In an earlier chapter I mentioned the audience response to his appearing in the stalls at the national theatre just before curtain up at the 1984 production of *Heartbreak House*. Getting on for ten years later, when he died, the streets of Athens and of towns throughout Greece were filled with people openly weeping at the news of his death. And as they wept they sang, unprompted, his poems in their musical settings. But I cannot imagine another Ritsos. The conditions that made him a hero to so many thousands of Greeks are unlikely to be repeated, any more than the kind of thugs and goons who in 1967 announced their mission 'to put Greece in plaster' are likely to occur again.

One of the prisons where Ritsos was held by the junta is at Nafplion, and there, just outside the perimeter walls, is a marble column on which is engraved lines he wrote to commemorate the political prisoners held there, and in which in my translation read

> May this place be sacred
> To the memory of those who suffered,
> Who trod here barefoot on the snake of tyranny,
> And with their blood wrote its history.

I mentioned my meeting with Ritsos, fleeting though it was, to Trypanis. And I said, half jokingly, that after I had shaken hands with the poet I had phoned my wife and told her I wouldn't be washing my right hand for weeks to come. Trypanis was not impressed. Nor was he impressed by any younger poets whose names I mentioned. Most were dismissed with an expansive shrug or a vigorous up-and-down motion of his massive head. When in conclusion I asked him what his overall view of contemporary Greek poetry was, he said, 'Great quantity. Little quality.'

I quoted those words to Andreas Angelakis a few nights later, when we met to talk about the article we might write for *Poetry Review*. Andreas had his own line in dismissive epigram. 'The sourness of the old and out-of-touch,' he said. In one important respect, Andreas was something of a hero. He was modern Greece's first openly gay poet, and in a country which was and still is dominated by an insistent masculinity and its attendant homophobia, it took real courage for Andreas to come out, which he had done two years earlier. At the time he was married. But with his declaration of gayness he left the family home, and though he remained on friendly enough terms with his wife and immediate family, or so he gave me to understand, he now lived alone in a flat in Piraeus, where he taught drama at a local high school. His announcement led to predictable consequences: hate mail and death threats, shit pushed through his letter-box, attempts to have him dismissed from his post. But through it all he remained resilient, wittily contemptuous of and to his persecutors. Soon after our first meeting, I went with a group of friends to his flat where he played us a recently-issued LP of songs he'd written for a group of singer-musicians. They were mostly love songs – 'S'*agapa*' – and had a wistful melancholy that he told me came in part from his experience of translating Turkish poetry.

Like most educated Greeks, Andreas was multi-lingual. He spoke good English, excellent French, he translated not merely from the Turkish but from German, and he was keen to know everything I could tell him about poetry in the UK. I lent him books and we were soon meeting on a regular basis. He translated some of my poems into Greek, where they appeared in various Greek journals, and in exchange I began to work at turning some of his poems into English. I was especially taken by a book-length sequence called *Ten Metaphysical Nights with Cavafy*, in which the narrator, himself a poet, tries imaginatively to recall the great Alexandrian poet's life, especially his early days, and even interviews his shade. After I returned to England we kept in touch, sending back and forth various drafts of the work-in-progress, and Andreas was planning to come to England to stay for a while so we could work together more concentratedly.

Then a letter came to say that he was ill and would have to put off his visit. Flu was mentioned, or a possible stomach upset. Weeks went by and I heard no more. Greek friends claimed not to know what was the matter. But then a woman friend, more candid than most, told me the news I dreaded to hear. Full-blown AIDS was the matter. I had hardly digested this news when further news arrived. Andreas was dead and his sparsely-attended funeral had already taken place. I think that is the only time I have felt real anger with Greek friends. Because the nature of Andreas's illness was to them one of unmentionable horror, they must have assumed that I would not want to hear about it or to mourn his death. But I did. Now, all I have left of our work together is the brief essay that appeared in *Poetry Review*, drafts of the *Cavafy* sequence, and my version of a poem by which he set much store, called 'Cartesian Logic', which was eventually published in an issue of *Modern Poetry in Translation*.

> Each body suffers its own hell,
> each scorches in its own fire;
> each body yearns in its own way,
> embraces with its own especial despair,
> forces love right up to death,
> forces it into a chamber with mirrors:
> who are you? Who is the other?
> And so you lie still, to be caressed like a corpse:
> the colour of the eyes changes, shifts to darker, to
> black, the mauve of loneliness, of the unfamiliar kiss.
>
> Each body has its own sweat,
> its own metaphysics.
> A pity, yet you need this game of words,
> abstractions, theories and the rest,
> otherwise you'll curse the flesh sleeping behind you,
> the unshaven face snoring by yours, totally unknown,
> after it's robbed you of your embrace and sperm.

The opening lines of this bleak, comfortless poem may seem prescient, but they are, I'm certain, to be read not as announcing the onset of the illness that was to kill Andreas, but as testifying to a deep, inner loneliness that sexual contact, far from ameliorating, makes more explicit.

Andreas's poetry is, I know, admired by Katerina Anghelaki-Rooke, a major poet who spends much of the year in Athens, though she has a family house on Aegina, which is where I first met her. It was another poet, Maria Servaki, who made the introductions. Maria lives a stone's throw away from the house in Athens where Seferis lived out his last years. It is in the district of Pagrati and near the old Olympic stadium in which the colonels assembled schoolchildren for parades so that they might learn to salute the Greek flag. (What else should they need to know?) She and Katerina had been students together, and although their paths began to diverge after Maria married the by all accounts decidedly eccentric Professor of English at Athens University, Bernard Blackstone, they kept in touch. Manos and Fotini, who live near Maria and know her well, took Pauline and me to meet her on an early summer's afternoon in 1985. The house we entered was cool and, with the shutters across to keep out the glaring heat, dark, so that at first we had some difficulty in making out the décor of the room into which we were shown. But as our eyes adapted to the gloom we became aware of what seemed to be numerous life size effigies of cats made out of various materials: they were posed on pedestals, on top of bookcases, draped across the back of chairs, curled up on side tables, stretched languorously on rugs. Then one moved.

Maria had no fewer than thirty-nine cats in the house. And if you're thinking that her house must therefore have stunk, then think again. I have known other women who chose to keep a large number of cats, and their houses did, it is true, smell overpoweringly of cat. So, invariably, did they. One, a colleague in the English department at Nottingham, where she inflicted her views on Spenser on anyone who came within earshot, whose affected eccentricities included an attempt to look like Edith Sitwell, and who was stupendously ridiculous in ways she didn't intend, stank of cat. Her clothes, her hair, her books: all, all of a piece throughout. I never went to her flat, but those who did came out reeling. Yet Maria's house smelt both clean and sweet. And all without the aid of air fresheners or artificial scents. An ioniser drew out stale air, but that apart, all was due to Maria's insistence that her cats maintain clean habits, that they ate only when and where she decreed, and that each should keep to its chosen place in the house. A small, dark, and intense woman, she was apparently the official 'cat-woman' of the city. Athens certainly needed one. At that time it was plagued by cats. As soon as you sat down to eat in a taverna a scrum of brawling cats would form round your feet. Others would leap onto adjacent chairs, some would scramble onto the table and nick food from bowls and plates. I love cats but I soon came to loathe the cats of Athens. One place in particular seemed a nightmare vision, a place of Gothic horror. Monastiraki Station, at the bottom of the Plaka, was a walk away from Syntagma Square, the city's main square, on one side of which is the old palace, now the parliament building, and on the other, cafés and bars. I would often take the train from my local stop, Victoria, alight at Monastiraki, then walk up to the square or veer right into the Plaka, where there were any number of small bars that I frequented, sometimes meeting friends, occasionally to be on my own. That was all fine.

Not so the station roof. The first time I found myself looking at it as I descended the steps from ground level to where it curved below me, I thought I had gone briefly mad. It couldn't, surely, be made of fur? But it was. From end to end cats hunkered down on its corrugated iron surface, a thick and seemingly unbroken covering that occasionally lifted like a slow wave or as though a wind had forced its way underneath – 'and the long carpets rose along the gusty floor' – whenever one or more groups of cats reformed themselves or made way for yet further cats. Why were they there? Perhaps because of the many tavernas and restaurants spread about the Plaka, and, when cats came off shift, this was their dormitory. Whatever the reason, I was glad when they finally and suddenly disappeared.

How were they got rid of? Poison, Maria told us. She didn't approve of suffering, but something had to be done, there were too many cats, the numbers had to be brought under control. She had had no part to play in the cleansing of Monastiraki, but she was nevertheless kept busy. Every day she expected to be called out to deal with injured, ill or dying cats, and to destroy litters of unwanted kittens. She undoubtedly loved cats – 'don't all poets?' she asked rhetorically – but she refused to be sentimental about them. Those in her care had without exception been rescued from certain death by her intervention and brought back to her house by her or delivered by well-wishers. Some had been run over, others had been mauled by dogs or rats, a few had fallen or been pushed onto the metro line below the pullulating roof of Monastiraki. Those too weak or badly injured to be saved were dispatched by injection. She showed us the black Gladstone bag which always went with her on her call-outs. Who contacted her? Anyone and everyone, she said. The mayor's office, police departments, private citizens, they all knew Maria. She was far more widely known as the 'cat-woman' than she was as a poet. As for her thirty-nine cats, each kept to its allotted place, attentive, and possessed of an almost unnerving calm. The four of us were seated on chairs arranged about the room, facing the chaise longue on which Maria sat bolt upright. I kept thinking that at least one of the cats would leap onto one of our laps, but no. They remained in their places.

Of course, I wanted to ask about her poetry. The collection she published in 1971, *The Other Garden*, had brought her some attention, its wild surrealism tempered by a rhetoric that seemed to owe something to Rilke. And yes, she said, Rilke was an influence on her, especially the *Duino Elegies*, but then wasn't he, weren't they, an influence on all later poets? Before I could answer that question, she added that Elytis was a stronger and more abiding influence, as was Nikos Karouzos. 'I am Greek, you see.' I thought of her strange, hectic poem 'Landscape of the Medusa and Chorus', very unlike the home lives of our own dear poets. I couldn't really claim to understand the poem and felt it very unlikely that she would in any way enlighten me. Anyway, it wasn't that sort of poem, was resistant to an irritable reaching after meaning, although its energy seemed to spring from a deep, erotic source. I had heard that she and Blackstone, whose study of Blake I once tried to read, had engaged in some pretty wild parties, but I couldn't really connect this severe woman, who remained seated throughout our visit, with either the poem or those legends about her earlier life.

As we prepared to leave I asked her if she still found time for poetry. Yes, she said, she wrote for two hours every day. And when might that be? Always between three and five in the morning. 'They are the hours I keep free. Nobody may disturb me then.'

There was one other question I wanted to put to her. Fotini had told me that in Maria's garden were tortoises aplenty. As it happened I was at the time putting together a selection of Lawrence's poetry and was intrigued by his six-poem sequence, *Tortoises*. This culminates in 'Tortoise Shout', which he describes as

> Worse than the cry of the new-born
> A scream,
> A yell, A shout,
> A paean,
> A death-agony,
> A birth-cry,
> A submission…
>
> So he tups, and screams
> Time after time that frail, torn scream…

Did male tortoises, I wondered, really make such a scream? Maria was briskly matter-of-fact. Yes, during copulation the male tortoise screamed. And screamed. 'You'd think it was having its penis ripped off.' She smiled slightly. Not so much Medusa, more Maenad.

From Maria to Katerina. My first meeting with her was a defining moment, even, if the word may be permitted, a revelation. Certainly, the atmosphere – ambience – surrounding her is one that seems nearer to true carnivalesque than any other I have ever come across. Her house on Aegina, built by a forebear early in the twentieth century, is a small, two-storey, neoclassical building, its rough-cast walls painted in the aubergine colour that is a feature of houses on the east side of the island but which I have seen nowhere else. As is common all over southern Europe, however, the house backs immediately onto the lane by means of which you approach it, while the front faces onto a large pistachio orchard, the harvested nuts a source of a variable though never considerable income. A first-floor balcony forms a perfect roof under which during summer evenings visitors sit at a long table to gaze at the blue shadows lengthening under gnarled bunchy trees, through which bats dart and flicker. People drift in to pay their respects, draw up whatever dilapidated chair is available, help themselves to beer, ouzo and local retsina with which the table is laden, and join in the talk and laughter, often raucous, much of it bawdy. And at the head of the table, Katerina conducts the talk or listens with voracious intensity to what others have to say, at her elbow what my friend the novelist Michael Wilding once called the biggest bottle of ouzo in the world, or, more likely nowadays, a glass of beer. Visiting poets often stay in what Katerina calls her garden 'bungalow': a converted outhouse that provides basic accommodation and may be inhabited whether or no she herself is in residence. At different times I have met there writers from Israel, Italy, France, the United States, the UK, and various of the old eastern European countries. Most if not all of these writers will be poets met on tour or at literary festivals, for more than any other contemporary Greek writer, Katerina, who despite a physical disability loves to travel, is in constant demand as a reader of her own work, and it seems hardly too much to call this demand world-wide. She once reluctantly turned down an offer to appear at the Tasmanian Poetry Festival, fearing the effects on her body of so long a flight, but she has been a welcome guest at festivals on all other continents. And I would imagine she has much the same effect on people wherever she goes. Wonder at the fineness of her poetry, its rhythmic largesse, its often erotic intensity, its deep linguistic resourcefulness – 'I serve the language' is a mantra of hers – and delight in her generous personality, her hospitable wit. And her laugh! A woman poet friend told me of a visit to a literary event in Thessaloniki. Alone on the first evening at a party where everyone seemed to know everyone else, she was standing in a corner surveying the scene when, from the other side of the vast room, she suddenly heard this laugh, 'on a rising note, and as though it contained all the warmth of the world. From what you'd told me about her I knew it had to be Katerina, so I went over and introduced myself. And she was, of course, completely welcoming. Wonderful company, the best.'

By the time that meeting took place, Shoestring Press had published *From Purple Into Night*, translated into English by Jackie Willcox, and with Pauline's lovely cover design, based on a drawing she did from an upstairs window of Katerina's house: a moon appearing from behind a pine tree. The book picked up a number of perceptive and enthusiastic reviews, none better than that by Rachel Hadas in the TLS, who remarked on its 'vivid specificity of detail as well as its honest portrayal of imaginative drought ... its note of clear, sensuous engagement with the worlds of the self, of the Greek landscape and of Greek (and other) mythology'. This is both just and exact, as is Hadas's noting that the poems manage a 'tranced evocation of girlhood ... their bald cries of pain'. Largely as a result of this review I had to reprint the first edition, orders for which came in from all parts of the globe. Some years later when I met Rachel Hadas on the island of Spetses, where she and I were appearing at a small poetry festival, I thanked her for her review, but she waved my thanks away. 'Whatever anyone writes of Katerina,' she said, 'is never likely to be adequate to what she is.' True.

At that festival on Spetses I met again Tassos Denegris, a poet whose *Selected Poems* the Press had just brought out in Philip Ramp's translation. Our first meeting had been a fleeting one, on Aegina, though not at Katerina's. Manos, who was friendly with Tassos's son, brought him to the Hotel Brown, where Pauline and I were staying for a couple of weeks. Manos hoped we would get on, but we didn't, not then. Tassos was in a black mood, smoked incessantly, spoke, if at all, in monosyllables, and soon left. Afterwards I wondered whether to make a poem out of that non-meeting of minds – the Hotel Brown is as it happens the *mis-en-scene* for a sequence of sour love poems by John Ash – but am glad now that I didn't. Because when we met two years later, also on the island, Tassos and I agreed to pretend that the previous meeting had never taken place; and this time it was fine.

Between the two meetings I had had time to revise my opinion of his poems. At first they seemed not merely slight but banal. Now, I could see that what I had taken for fragments of reportage were in fact properly epigrammatic, and that the poems were at their best laced with a teasing, slightly off-centre laconic tinct. As a result, I'd agreed to Phil's proposal for a *Selected*, which he would translate. Hence, the purpose of Tassos's visit. We were to discuss publication of the work, which was, Phil told me, more or less finished. Pauline and I now had our own small flat at the village of Faros, just round the corner from Phil and Sarah's house. We all agreed to meet at a local taverna where both wine and food were good and the view over the Saronic Gulf unimprovable. Tassos arrived, beaming, with a new partner. I remembered him as dark-haired but he was now greying, although in other ways he seemed, for all his slight stoop and his thin body, younger. With his glasses and his wry smile, he looked somehow like a small, perky owl, one that didn't bother to go hunting, safe in the knowledge that food would come to him. As it did. For Joanna, all long dark-brown hair, vivacious, mobile features, was scrupulously attentive to Tassos's needs – she cut up his food for him, even lifted morsels to his lips – while she herself ate hardly anything, preferring to smoke cigarette after cigarette.

Tassos had not long returned from reading at the Cambridge Festival, where he had been particularly impressed, he told me, by Ken Smith and Roy Fisher. What did I think of them? Two terrific poets, I said, and Roy was something of a friend. Did Tassos know that he was a fine jazz pianist?

He didn't, registered the fact, but told me that he preferred rock music, and mentioned as especial favourites a group called The Grateful Dead. Never mind, he was beguiling company. Magnificently sure of his opinions – 'Polish poetry is very good, French poetry apart from Jacottet is, I may say, rubbish' – he told me that as a younger man he had spent years in Italy following football. 'I was, I think you say, a football hooligan.'

'Really?' I found that difficult to credit. Tassos was at best middle-height and, judging from a body on which there was still precious little flesh, as a young man he'd have surely been far too slight to risk getting involved in a fight.

'I took a fork to football matches, you know. That I jabbed into the backs of opposing fans, then ran way before they could catch me.'

'And they never did catch you?'

A shrug, that Greek shrug which is the most expressive in the world: full of weariness, of acceptance, but which is also unbowed. 'Sometimes.'

The shrug was in full working order when Tassos and Joanna stood on the doorstep of our house in Nottingham early one February evening the following year. The *Selected Poems* was now in print and I had arranged some readings for Tassos, which was why they were here. But that didn't explain their dress. The pair of them were in summer clothes, shivering, so cold they could hardly speak, while behind them snow fell and the temperature held steady at somewhere below zero.

I got them inside, poured whiskies. 'Why on earth haven't you brought winter coats?'

'The skies were blue in Athens,' Tassos said, when he had thawed out sufficiently to manage a few words. 'It was warm. Seventy degrees.'

'But this is England.'

There came the shrug. 'Yes,' Tassos agreed, 'this is England.'

The previous December Lydia Stephanou had also been forced to experience the vagaries of the English climate. Lydia was in London to launch the English version of her book-length poem *Landscapes from the Origin and The Wandering of Yk*. This strange, phantasmagoric narrative, part metaphysical, part psychological, wholly surrealistic, had first been published in Greece in 1965, and is at some level about the modern Greek sense of alienation and the struggle to find some basis for a secure sense of selfhood at a time and in a place where this seems impossible to achieve. ('Wherever I move, Greece wounds me'.) Philip had made a translation of the poem which I offered to publish, at the same time undertaking to bring out his version of some of Manolis Anagnostakis's poems, and the *Odes* of Andreas Kalvos.

Philip filled me in about Anagnostakis. He'd been born in Thessaloniki in 1925, was a life-long member of the communist party, and in the post-war chaos had been imprisoned and at one point came within hours of execution. (I think the first of his twelve published collections was in fact written while he was incarcerated.) Perhaps for this reason many saw in him a kind of heroic idealism that they would probably have called Byronic. Certainly his poems had at their best a raw power and, from time to time, a sardonic eye-cocked look at contemporary events that made them well worth publishing, at all events in Philip's versions.

But it was Kalvos who most interested me. A contemporary of Solomos, Greece's nationalist poet (Kalvos was born in Zante in 1792 and died in 1869), he wanted to emulate him. But although he hoped that his poems, first published in Geneva in 1824, would help inspire his countrymen who were then engaged in the war of liberation, he was to be disappointed. This isn't to be wondered at, though it seems to have taken him by surprise. Kalvos, living in exile, wrote in a hybrid Greek that very few could understand. The Greek soldiers among whom his *Odes* were distributed by philhellene friends scratched their heads, laughed, and then got on with fighting the Turks. As for Kalvos, who had apparently been anticipating a triumphant return to his native land, he remained in exile, eventually dying in London. But the translations George made of Kalvos while working on his doctoral thesis so intrigued me that I suggested he do more of them, especially as we discovered that Kalvos had never before been translated into English. They were difficult, yes, dense, sometimes impenetrably so, but I was taken by their impacted lyricism, above all, perhaps, by a registering of natural phenomena that is also richly metaphoric.

For the first and only time, I decided to use a Greek printer, simply because it meant proofs wouldn't have to be entrusted to the mercies of the Greek and British postal systems, and all three translations were first 'presented' in Athens on an evening when the British Ambassador put in an appearance. Hospitality was lavish. There was much food and drink. The Ambassador, having been formally introduced to the hundred or so guests, made a brief speech, I spoke merely to introduce the poets and translators, and then we got down to the evening's business. Lydia read in Greek, as did George, and Phil read some of Anagnostakis's poems in both Greek and English. (The poet himself was in attendance, tall, dignified, but old, enfeebled, and unable to stand for any length of time.) After that, the plan was to eat, to drink, to mingle, and to buy copies of the books.

Unfortunately, we had reckoned without the man who had been chosen – or had appointed himself, I never found out which – to make the closing remarks.

He began by telling everyone that he himself was a writer. A dramatist, yes, but he was now at work on his autobiography. This apparently owed something to the inspiration of James Joyce – *Finnegan's Wake* was mentioned – although our man had taken Joyce's playful experimentation further than the Irishman would have thought possible. He therefore proposed to give us some examples of his linguistic virtuosity. Three quarters of an hour later he was still at it. By then at last half the audience had left and those who remained were numbed into sullen catatonia. The book sales that evening were minimal.

I was damned if I'd allow that to happen in London. I said as much when I met Lydia the following day in her apartment, just behind Konalaki Square. Her husband, an ex-ambassador, was present, and over lunch we talked of his various postings, including one in Australia where Lydia had become friendly with that fine and under-regarded Australian poet, Rosemary Dobson. But Lydia's great passion was for French poetry of the later nineteenth century. She had made a study of the Decadence, quoted at length from Laforgue, Verlaine, and above all Rimbaud, and as she talked it became clear that the poet of *Le Bateau Ivre* meant more to her, perhaps, than any other poet, certainly more than I had realised when I first read her own work. At that time Lydia was, I guess, in her late sixties, slim, almost petite, and in her elegant surroundings, and with food on the table that was, let's say, international in disposition, and accompanied by fine French wines, she seemed the least Greek Greek I had met.

She retained that elegance in London. Having over several visits to the Hellenic Foundation on Brooke Street become friendly with the gorgeously dramatic person who ran it – her manner of descending a staircase would have had Bette Davis signing up for her correspondence course – I persuaded her to take on the English launch of the three Shoestring books. Although there was no question of Anagnostakis making the trip, and Phil was otherwise engaged, Lydia came. So did George, bringing with him a friend, a plumber who limped up the

Foundation steps – apparently in his desperation to get to Soho as soon as they arrived (*why* wasn't explained, though I could guess) he nearly fell under a tube train. There was a good attendance, including many London-based Greeks, the wine which the Director supplied flowed freely and, shorn of unnecessary speeches, the evening passed off well. I even sold a large number of books.

Afterwards, a sizeable group of us crowded into a nearby Italian restaurant. Among the party was a young Greek poet, Dimitris Lyacos, then living in London, who had been dragooned into attending the launch even though he claimed to be depressed. I had heard him offer this excuse when the Director phoned to require his presence. 'Depressed?' she said incredulously. 'We are *all* depressed. *I* am depressed. But you will come.'

He came. He even joined in when George, later on, decided that now was the time for *rembetika*. And so for half an hour a packed Italian restaurant near Oxford Street echoed to songs I had last heard at Babi's. True, there was here no musical accompaniment, but George's surprisingly full bel canto voice hardly required one.

When he finished, the diners broke into spontaneous applause. A waiter brought an extra carafe of wine to our table.

'A reward for your singing,' he said to George and smiled round at our table.

George accepted the offering with a gracious bow. Then he shook the waiter's hand.

'I sing better in Greece,' he said.

Cultural Anthropology

'Any Greek wants to own his own shop'
    Costa explains. I test his chair
then sit as he pours the last drop
    of ouzo. 'For you' he begs, 'here!'

pushing across a plate of mezes.
    'Go on, eat. This bloody machine,
it don't work properly, these days,'
    and he grins, oil bearding his chin.

Another customer looms at the door.
    'Tomorrow,' Costa promises, 'but please
come in.' Table goods hit the floor –
    'Hey, sit here. Beer? Sardines then? Cheese?'

A woman I know says every Greek
    male is mannerless and lacks ambition:
'I may sound bitter, but I speak
    from experience. I married one.'

Costa presides hospitably
    over his wreck of a laundry. Before long
he'll close and take the day's money
    to a bouzouki. There, wet-eyed with song,

and, if luck lasts, a woman,
    he'll curse the gods who've thrown him down:
then it's home to his parents again,
    to dream the pebble under his apt tongue.

CHAPTER SEVEN

A Winter Wedding

I GOT BACK TO ATHENS at the start of the new year, 1985. The morning after my arrival, and following a roistering evening at Babi's when I may have made rather too apparent my feeling that while the taverna probably hadn't missed me I had certainly missed it, I tried to do what I'd been unable to accomplish on the day of my departure for England. Early on a mid-December morning, I had wanted to deposit most of my 498,000 drachms in the Commercial Bank of Greece, which had a branch next door to No 9? The bank, however, was on strike, the front door blocked by a military policeman in olive-grey uniform who was cradling a sub-machine gun. Odd. Policemen are meant to prevent people getting away with cash they're not entitled to. This one was preventing me from handing in cash that I'd earned. I thought about walking further along Acharnon Street to a branch of the National Bank, but decided against it. I'd little enough time to get to the airport, and besides, a previous visit to the bank in question hadn't persuaded me it was a good place with which to do business.

That visit had occurred shortly after I'd first arrived in Athens. Before leaving England I'd arranged for some money to be transferred from my UK bank to the one with which it had, so my branch manager told me, 'an arrangement'. The nature and even fact of the arrangement was clearly news to the man at the front desk of the National Bank, Acharnon Street, when Pauline and I called on him. He knew nothing of any money in my name having been received at the branch office where we now sat, and this, despite the fact that I bore in my hand a letter insisting that the transaction had taken place. After much consulting of files he made some lengthy and, it seemed, inconclusive telephone calls, which were followed by equally lengthy, equally inconclusive discussions with other employees, all of them requiring a good deal by way of the kind of gesture which Cicero characterised as rhetorical pronunciation – raised eyebrows, wide-splayed hands, outthrust underlip – and, in the manager's case, extravagant use of a cigarette as wand, baton, poniard. At the end of a dramatic dialogue with one cashier (she had been called from a booth in front of which, as the debate wound on, a long line of customers grew increasingly mutinous-looking), he asked us whether we would like to take a coffee. Coffee, yes, that would be good.

Another telephone conversation was followed by a rather blank twenty minutes during which the manager smoked two further cigarettes and rummaged through his desk – 'looking for inspiration,' Pauline whispered – and we assumed our acceptance of coffee had been misunderstood as rejection. Then, in through the street door came a man who gripped a metal ring from which depended three chains connected at their bottom end to a round steel tray about sixteen inches across. The man at the desk broke into smiles. 'Coffee,' he said, reaching out to the tray and taking from it two acorn-sized cups which he placed in front of us. The bearer of the tray retreated and we drank our coffee.

A little later, and after yet another telephone conversation, the manager announced that he had finally located what might be the money my bank had sent over from England, although it had been deposited in an entirely different branch, one that he gave us to understand was on the far side of Athens.

'But the money can presumably be re-routed to this branch?'

A shrug. 'That will take time.'

'How long?'

'A week. Maybe two weeks.'

'But how can it take so long? Why can't you simply phone and ask for the money to be transferred at once?'

Well, because he couldn't. Nor could he provide me with a chequebook. He seemed taken aback that I should even ask for one. Did I not know they were rarely used? No, I said, I didn't, I was new to his country. A shrug. Never mind, the shrug said, you will come to understand our ways. The most he could promise was that he would make enquiries to discover whether it would be at all possible to provide me with such a thing. To be fair, he did and it was. But when, some weeks later, I dropped in at the bank to collect the chequebook I'd been informed was now available, it turned out to be a set of twelve grease-proof half-pages, roughly cut and with a Greek name crossed through and mine superimposed. At all events, I assumed I must be the Mr Loukas identified as the 'book's' new owner. One look at it made plain the sheer unlikeliness of anyone ever accepting a cheque that would have to be freed by main force from the massive staples that clamped the pages together. But by then I had realised that there was no point in trying to pay for anything by cheque. Nobody else did, and I couldn't hope to succeed where they scorned to go. And so, my money having finally crossed the city, I withdrew it from the local branch and thereby closed an account I had never really opened.

So no, the National Bank of Greece wasn't for me. But nor, it turned out on that raw morning in January, 1985, was the Commercial Bank. For having retrieved the money which over the Christmas period had been deposited in various hiding places about my flat, I now found I couldn't deposit it in the bank next door. The same policeman who'd barred my entry some three weeks earlier was there, maintaining his guard. 'Still on strike?'

He shook his head. This was apparently a different strike.

I went back to my flat and once more set about distributing bundles of notes in different places. Why, you may wonder, had I simply not taken most of it home with me at Christmas and deposited it in my Nottingham bank? Two reasons. One, the drachm was such a weak currency that what passed for a reasonable salary in Greece was a pittance elsewhere and so worth very little once translated into pounds sterling. Two, the Greek government, having become alarmed at the drain of capital from Greece, had recently passed a law preventing anyone from taking more than twenty thousand drachms out of the country. And while Customs at Athens airport was virtually non-existent – there was a joke to the effect that, provided you remembered to wrap it in brown paper, you could pass unchallenged beneath the noses of the officials with an elephant tucked under your arm –

they could, as the Fulbright professor said, smell money. Already an American priest, intercepted with some eighty thousand drachms in his suitcase as he was about to board a plane for New York, was languishing in jail, and I had no intention of joining him there. So while I was away for Christmas the drachms stayed in the flat. And it now appeared that they would have to stay there for some time yet. I finished stowing the money and then headed in the direction of my local friendly laundry man.

I found Dimitris in a melancholy mood. He explained that in a month's time he was to re-marry. Then why so pale and wan, fond lover? The anticipation of such an event ought to prompt rejoicing, not black despair. Yes, Dimitris said, but his parents disapproved, and he feared their displeasure. Then, rousing himself, he told me that in half-an-hour's time he would close the shop for lunch. Could I meet him in the next-door *kafeneion*, and he would then explain all?

The *kafeneion* where we sat hunched over fish stew is of a kind that has now more or less disappeared. Such *kafeneions* were attended exclusively by men, who came at any hour of the day to talk, to smoke, to play *tavli* (backgammon), to drink and eat cheaply, to while away long hours of what frequently would have been an otherwise unemployed existence. A mixture of soup kitchen, greasy spoon and working men's club, the *kafeneion* was, as far as I know, unique to Greece, but an older Greece. Even in the '80s younger men were beginning to take themselves to bars or cafés such as the Medusa, where the seating was more comfortable, the range of drinks wider, the dress more fashionable, the music more international (for which read 'pop'), and where women were welcome.

'It's Aleka you're marrying, I take it?'

Yes, it was Aleka, his childhood sweetheart. I had met her on several occasions before Christmas, an attractive if tempestuous woman with a loud laugh and a convulsive way with a cigarette, which she seemed able to dispose of in two or at most three intakes of breath. Several of her teeth were broken or missing, courtesy of a drunken bully of a husband, a policeman from whom she was now divorced, but by whom she had earlier borne a boy, Christos, now some five years old, who was usually with her, even on late-evening visits to Babi's. As for Dimitris, he was a widower. His wife, George had told me months earlier, had died from blood poisoning brought on by a dog bite, and had left him with two children, a boy and girl, who now lived with his parents. I had met both parents and children one November evening when Dimitris took me and an English friend then staying with me to the family home on the northern edge of Athens. He wanted us to experience good Greek home cooking, and that evening we did.

Not that there was anything wrong with Manolis's, at all events if you excused one attempt to bake cod in what he claimed was a special Egyptian sauce that tasted like nothing so much as rancid custard. But Dimitris's mum was in a different league. That evening she provided tomatoes stuffed with the most delicately flavoured rice, in which aromatic herbs played their part as they exploded gently against the roof of your mouth, *spetsefia* (a succulent dish of octopus baked in oil with spinach leaves), small cheese pies that melted on the tongue, *pasticchio* of a sumptuous nature whose equal I never found in a taverna, not even Babi's, neither too dry nor too moist, the pasta cooked until it had just the right measure of resistance, lamb cutlets seasoned with rosemary and sprinkled with lemon juice to bring out their savour, and, of course, a large bowl of Greek salad remarkable for home-cured black olives and cucumber so sweet of taste and so fleshy you could have sworn it was the rarest kind of fruit. And when all was ready and the men were served, Dimitris's mum, together with the sister who had helped her prepare this feast and Dimitris's young daughter, retired to the kitchen, while the men, including Dimitris's son, ate and drank the retsina that Dimitris's father supplied. Whether it was his own retsina I don't know, but he certainly brewed the bottle of what turned out to be skin-blisteringly strong raki with which he sent us away, a hand raised in salutation, his tall, lean frame with iron-grey hair and moustache under splendidly beaked nose virtually filling the doorway and allowing little room for his wife, who bore an uncanny resemblance to Hylda Baker, to wave her farewells.

'Wonderful,' I said, as the three of us drove back into Athens, 'but I feel guilty your mother chose not to join us at table.'

'She is a Greek mother,' Dimitris said, 'she don't eat with the men.'

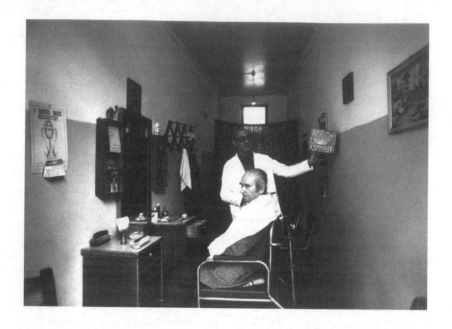

She was a Greek mother in other ways too, he now told me, pushing aside his fish stew and reaching for a cigarette. It was she who long ago had objected to his adolescent love affair with Aleka, insisting that they go their separate ways. Aleka's parents were poor, there was even a rumour that her mother had at one time been on the streets, and whatever the truth or otherwise of this rumour, Aleka was not good enough for Dimitris. Therefore he must not marry her.

As Dimitris told me this, adding that his mother would never deviate from her assurance that he was too good for the likes of Aleka, that he had some sort of destiny to fulfil, I realise that he was the perfect exemplar of a joke Manos once told me. What are the five proofs that Jesus was Greek? 1. He worked in his father's shop (The laundry where Dimitris worked had indeed been owned by his father), 2. He didn't leave home until he was thirty (Dimitris left home when he was twenty-five, but still…), 3. He thought he was God, 4. His mother thought he was God, 5. He thought his mother was a virgin. And now the virgin mother was appalled that her god-like son was marrying the Magdalene. 'I am worried, in my heart I feel pain, and my head, it hurts,' he said, hitting both in turn with the flat of his hand. 'They are poisoning my children's minds. They tell them I am a bad man, and they try to keep me from them. They don't want me to see them.'

'Oh, surely not.'

But Dimitris thumped the *kafeneion* table. 'I tell you true,' he said. 'I do not lie. Listen, you must to know what happened at Christmas. It was terrible.' And as he told me, I felt that for once he was barely exaggerating.

He had decided to take the newly-divorced Aleka, with whom he was now openly living in a small apartment near his shop, together with Christos, to meet his parents. A risky move, without doubt, but he hoped that once his mother saw Christos, who was a loveable little lad, her stern resolve not to allow Aleka into her family would melt away and, even if the meeting wasn't to be all hearts and flowers, they could at least greet each other civilly, could agree to be on friendly terms. And so, confident that he could to some extent win his mother round, Dimitris phoned her to say he was on his way with his bride-to-be and her son.

But there was no rapprochement. His mother met him at the front door and refused him entry to the house. Could he speak to his father? Absolutely out of the question, and besides she had sent him off for the day. (I pictured the old man cowering upstairs, terrified lest Dimitris should try to force his way in and he be ordered to do his duty and repel his son and the 'whore'.) The argument became shrill, turned to open invective, curses and oaths were vigorously exchanged, and Dimitris, together with Aleka and a bewildered and tearful Christos, had finally to beat a retreat.

Later the same evening, still hoping for the best, he phoned his mother, only to be told that she was casting him off forever for associating with a woman who would bring nothing but shame on the family, and that as he was no longer a fit person to act as parent to his children she would try to get them adopted as wards of court.

'But surely she can't do that?'

'She can make them not want to see me again.'

'Then I'm truly sorry,' was all I could think to say.

Dimitris studied me, and as he did so, the look of settled despondency shifted, became less secure, and it really was as though clouds were passing away from the clear light that now began to spark in his eyes.

'But, my old friend,' he said, 'we will be happy. And perhaps in time my mother will be happy, too. I see blue skies for us all.' He stood up, suddenly animated, where a moment earlier he had slumped at the table. 'And you must come to the party we have before the wedding. Aleka's father, he wants to meet you.'

All Greeks are able to move from dark to light and back again with uncanny speed, but nobody I have met could equal Dimitris, either in range or the rapidity of his changes.

> As high as we have mounted in delight
> In our dejection do we sink as low

And Wordsworth had never seen Dimitris. With the black dog shaken off, he required a beer, then another. Then another. By the time he was due back at his laundry he was flying.

The night before the wedding George collected me and we walked the short distance to the apartment where Aleka's father lived alone, his wife either having died or disappeared. (I never found out which.) As tall as Dimitris's father, with very much the same kind of grand moustache sprouting under his emphatic nose, he was without his left arm, which had been amputated at the shoulder, and during the course of the evening used the right arm to corral most of the bottles that came within reach. While the rest of the small group of friends ate food Aleka had prepared – she proved almost as good a cook as Dimitris's mother, and her *spetsefia*, made with spicy sausage rather than octopus, was if anything even better – the old boy drank and, fixing each of us in turn with his glittering eye, conducted an unbroken series of monologues from which I recall the anathematising of the previous administration of New Democracy (for raising the price of toilet paper), the unfailing ingratitude of the young to their elders (this, though all the evening's drink had been supplied by Dimitris), and his own role in defeating Hitler. (Essential: without him Greece would still be in bondage to the Nazis.)

As we walked home, I remarked to George that Aleka's father had presumably lost his arm in battle. 'No,' George said, 'an accident at work.'

Early next afternoon, having put on a clean shirt and added a tie bought especially for the occasion, I headed for the nearby church where the nuptials were to be performed. It was in a small square surrounded by laurel bushes, in one of which I found Dimitris's mother lurking. She came forward to greet me and I saw that she had been crying, and that her eyes were still wet. 'I will only go in there if I can go with you,' she said, passing a hand across her face before taking a grip on my arm.

'Of course,' I said, and as I did so Aleka's father passed us without so much as a nod of recognition, mounted the four or five marble steps before the church's entrance, and disappeared within.

We followed, and as soon as my eyes had become accustomed to the dim light filtering through the tall stained-glass windows, I saw George, spruce in a what looked to be a new two-piece suit, standing before the altar, Dimitris beside him, equally spruce and a good deal taller and broader of shoulder. Those shoulders were all muscle. Glancing at them I realised again how formidably strong Dimitris was, and thought, too, of his dextrous-fingered skill at handling engines and all mechanical things: he had once taken down an old-fashioned and faulty roller-blind of mine that I found too heavy to budge, repaired and replaced it, and all without evident strain or even the need to remove from his lips the lit cigarette that he smoked throughout such demanding manoeuvres; and I know that he uncomplainingly shifted for others pieces of machinery that they found immovable. Not that any of these others had put in an appearance at church. A few, a very few, of Aleka's friends were to the left of the aisle, as was her father, so I steered Dimitris's mum to a pew on the right. We had it to ourselves.

A slightly dishevelled priest now appeared through the iconostasis (George later confirmed that he was drunk), Aleka, whose entrance I'd missed, came forward to stand beside Dimitris, and the ceremony began. There was an intricate passage which required Dimitris and Aleka to follow the priest round the altar table, three times if I remember rightly, pursued by George, whose function it was to keep hold of wreaths he had previously placed on their heads. As the four of them went round and round it became obvious that George, being a good deal shorter than either Dimitris or Aleka, was in considerable difficulty, even though, or perhaps because, he went tiptoe, and at one point he tripped and nearly fell.

After that, those of us in the pews were handed rose petals and instructed to throw them over the bride and groom. Problem. In an attempt to comfort and console Dimitris's mother, who had been trembling and moaning to herself throughout the ceremony, I had put my left arm round her shoulders, which meant that I was forced to receive rose petals into my free right hand. I am, however, entirely left-handed, with the result that when I tried to throw the rose petals over Aleka and Dimitris they merely ascended in a gentle parabola and then came fluttering down onto my own upturned face. Still my gaucherie was not without its compensations. Dimitris's mother, who had previously been the tragic philosopher, now found cheerfulness entering in.

The church part of the ceremony having been completed, we formed up on the steps outside before the happy pair led a very short procession back to Aleka's father's apartment, dispensing as they went sugared almonds to the few onlookers who were on the streets at that time of afternoon. Arriving at the apartment door, I kissed Aleka and Dimitris on both cheeks, wished them luck, presented them with the gift I had brought with me – a water jug made of crystal glass, beautifully wrapped and tied in ribbon by the shopwoman from whom I'd bought it – and left them.

I would like to be able to report that the marriage prospered. Alas, Dimitris and Aleka had scarcely been married a week before rows of increasing severity began to break out between them, and by the time I left Greece some six months later their relationship was as good as dead. I liked them both but looking back I can see that their marriage never stood a chance. Too much had happened to each since the days of their adolescent love affair. There was, for example, Dimitris's guilt over his children, whom he was certainly allowed to see – his mother relented to that extent at least – but from whom she continued to bar Aleka. There was Aleka's little boy, Christos, who, despite being a delightful child, not unreasonably showed signs of resenting the close attention Dimitris paid to his mother. And then there was the fact that Dimitris, who had been a widower for a number of years, didn't much take to the inevitable demands of family life. He wanted to be out with his friends, to spend as he thought fit whatever money the laundry brought in, to eat and drink the night away and, if he didn't feel like work, to abandon the shop for days at a time. One night, during a swelling argument at a taverna, he suddenly grabbed an empty bottle and broke it over his own head. That happened after I had left and I knew about it only because George phoned to tell me the story. 'It is over,' he said. 'They cannot live together.' I wasn't sure whether he meant that the bottle breaking had a symbolic significance. (Wasn't plate smashing nowadays just plate smashing, something that the owners of non-echt tavernas encouraged tourists to do?)

But that evening marked the end. By the following Christmas Aleka was once again living with her father, a pinching existence from which, so George informed me some years later, she was rescued by a 'sea-captain', an older man who became her third husband. As for Dimitris, he resumed his bachelor existence.

Faith and Reason: An Aeginetan Dialogue

For Gerald Thompson

Near the top of that boulder-clogged
Pine-dark path, you said, a scold
Nun appeared to thwart your progress.
'What are you doing here and why?'
'Searching, Sister, I've been told

Of pure views not far ahead.'
'Such foolishness! And don't you know
You risk your life from vicious snakes
Clustered across this path you tread?
Go back at once to your ways below.'

'Sister, I have a walking stick!'
'What then?' Time for the *coup de grace*.
'The wood was cut on Holy Mountain, Sister!'
A winning smile. 'And do you
Think our snakes know *that*, you ass?'

CHAPTER EIGHT

Easter and Aegina

IN MARCH 2005 the American poet Michael Waters sent me an inscribed copy of his *Parthenopi: New and Selected Poems*. Michael had spent a year at Nottingham University in the early 1970s, where I had taught him and, as then publisher of the Byron Press, had brought out an apprentice pamphlet of his poems, *A Rare Breed of Antelope*. Over the years we'd never quite lost touch, and I knew that at some time in the 1980s he'd been in Greece. Now, in a letter that accompanied *Parthenopi*, he told me that 'one of my favorite routines while living in Athens was to take the ferry to Aegina, rent a bicycle, then pedal to Perdika for lunch.'

Given the mishaps that surrounded my first visit to the island, I might have chosen never to go back. But I decided that the curse of Spetses didn't extend to Aegina, and from the early autumn of '84 I took to slipping over there as often as I could. As Michael's letter implies, you could easily get there and back in half a day – less, if need be. I had merely to walk to the station at Victoria Square, which was no more than a hundred yards away from my flat, take the metro down to Piraeus, cross the road, board one of the ferries that plied regularly between the port and the island, and an hour and a half later I would be stepping ashore to confront what, after so many years and innumerable visits and protracted stays on Aegina, is a scene that never fails to lift my heart. At the head of the quay is the three-storey biscuit-coloured customs building, dilapidated but still handsome, in front of it a line of gaily decorated, open horse-drawn carriages that will take the visitor at a fast trot along the waterfront or, if preferred, plod about the town's back streets; curving gently away to the right, a row of shops, tavernas, the fish market and *ouzeries* that stretch as far as a church framed by palm trees, and beyond, a large, elegantly square, white-painted mansion which is in fact Hotel Brown. Hotel Brown faces onto the town beach. Nowadays increasingly scruffy, the beach in the autumn of 1984 was clean and well-swept, and, on the few occasions I could spare the time and, more important, money, I would book in for an overnight stay at the hotel. From there, I could swim.

The best time for swimming was early morning. The water, though chill, had an opalescent shimmer to it and was so clear that I could see small fish flickering about between, behind, below my body, or, it seemed at a whim, curving up from the sea's surface, as many as forty or fifty of them at a time, in a shallow ellipsis, swarf slivers glittering in the sun.

Even at that hour I did not have the place to myself. As I have previously mentioned, early morning was when a flock of old ladies would come down to the beach, chattering like starlings, slowly remove their voluminous dresses, and then as slowly wade out to sea. It didn't matter where I chose to put my towel, the old ladies would always surround me. Sometimes, but by no mean always, they wished me good morning. Their behaviour was, I came to realise, prompted by the same instinct for hospitality that told habitués of Babi's that no person should be left to eat alone, as I never was. If I wanted to avoid them, I had therefore to retreat to the garden of Hotel Brown, a most beautiful, shady place of acacia trees, curved stone benches and tables with, all about, artfully arranged amphorae, variously atilt as well as upstanding, plus the model of a small boat, stripped down to its bare ribs. The Brown family's money, I discovered, had initially come from sponge, although whether they sent their ships across the Aegean to Kalymnos, where the best sponges were to be found, I don't know.

But before I got paid, the extravagance of a night spent on Aegina was out of the question. I didn't even think to hire a bicycle, as Michael did, although I once walked down to Perdika (it means Partridge), a small fishing village at the foot of the island about eight miles from the port town of Aegina itself, and with a number of excellent fish tavernas that stretch alongside its harbour wall. In later years Pauline and I took especial pleasure in inviting friends to go with us by bus to Perdika, where we could eat, swim, and then, following the suggestion of a chalk-written notice advertising boat rates, pay a boatman to take us back to the port town by caique. The journey by water took about half an hour, although you couldn't always be sure that you would leave on time. On one occasion, when I needed to be back by five o'clock, I arranged with a Captain Georgios that he would be at his boat at four p.m., ready and waiting to take us. Could he guarantee that? Of course, of course. No problem.

The arrangement confirmed and some money handed over, we went off to swim, to enjoy a long, leisurely lunch, and then at four o'clock we presented ourselves at Captain Georgios's boat. Of Captain Georgios there was, however, no sign. Nor was there half an hour later. Nor did I know where to find him. Shortly afterwards another man, someone I didn't at all recognise, came running up. 'You are waiting for Captain Georgios?'

Yes, we were.

'No good. He can't to come. I am to take you. Please to get in.'

As we clambered aboard the caique I asked, 'What's happened? Is Captain Georgios all right? Has he had an accident?'

'No, not accident.' The stand-in skipper shook his head vehemently. 'Captain Georgios,' he said, as he started up the motor, 'he has fallen into the arms of a woman.'

My first visits to Aegina were half-day ones. I'd step off the ferry, pause to admire the customs house, then choose one of the waterfront cafés at which to sit, order a beer and a sandwich, and spend two or three hours gazing over the water, trying to read whatever book I'd brought with me, after which I'd stroll about the backstreets, then make my way down to the quay to await a Piraeus-bound ferry. Nothing strenuous, nothing out-of-the-way, but always something for the eye to relish, something to reward what Henry James called 'the gaping habit before life'. It might be the dove-grey light over the nearby island of Agistri, or a man with the smallest motorbike in the world determined to fit onto it not merely himself but an enormous roll of carpet. Or it might be the piratical-looking figure, dressed all in dark blue, occasionally to be seen striding along the waterfront, a parrot on one shoulder and on the other a falcon. Or, more rarely, but it happened, there might be a frigate bird moving improbably about the harbour's water, like an oversized bath-toy, or a group of fishermen crouched beside their boats and exchanging tales of the ones that got away from last night's catch, their accounts made eloquent by their extravagant, ritualistic gestures. Above all, there was the light: a luminous blue and gold in which everything was held and clarified as though by some achieved alchemical process.

My favourite café was called Bessie's, partly because it had an elegant, wood-panelled interior, with a mezzanine floor from which, in the worst weather, you could look down on the swirl of activity beneath, and partly because from outside, where, unless the weather prohibited it, I always sat, the view across to Agistri and beyond was – well, enchanting is a dull word but I don't know another as accurate. *Enchant: to put under a spell, bewitch.* Yes, that's about the size of it. Certainly, no book I took with me could hope to compete with it. Shortly after arriving in Athens I read Dilys Powell's touching memoir of her return to immediate post-war Greece (the account of her years on Crete in the 1930s, *The Villa Ariadne*, ought never to be allowed out of print), in which she confesses that she took plenty of books to read and invariably found herself raising her eyes from the printed page and hardly ever dropping them again, and I know just what she means. Wherever you look, there is so much to capture the eye that you simply want to go on looking. 'And where you love you cannot break away'. Adapt that line of John Wain's to 'And where you look you cannot break away', and you have it. 'Greeks love beauty,' my friend the Greek-Australian poet, Dimitris Tsaloumas, once said to me, and there was such vehemence about his words that I knew he felt himself to be speaking a deep, ungainsayable truth. At that moment we were standing on a beach of his native Leros, and I was aware, as he plainly wasn't, that all around us were rusty tins, shattered bottles, and the detritus you associate with rubbish tips rather than with a cared-for coastline. But Dimitris was staring into the distance, towards where, beyond an indigo-blue sea, and screened by nacreous mist, Patmos lay. The near view didn't interest him.

But how to render the far view? *Any* view of Greece, if it comes to that? The artist Andreas Foukas, who has lived on Aegina for some twenty years, talks good sense on the subject. Most painters, he says, and especially those who come from northern Europe, think that to capture Greek land- or sea-scape you have to be as impressionistic or indefinite as possible. Northern artists try to render iridescence, a play of light that hints at infinite space and is not anchored to particularities. Hopeless. Greek landscape is geometric. It is a matter of sharply defined lines, of mountains cut cleanly against sky, of terraced fields that are rhomboid or variously rectilinear, of deep valleys, crevasses, of houses and churches shaped by light so clear that it shaves away all imprecision. As to colour, Andreas uses five basic colours for landscapes which are far and away the most compelling visual statement I know of how Greece – well, Aegina – actually looks, though it's only when you study his work you see how and why he has caught that look. Above all, he will not use blue. No, he says, grey against black, or against green, or yellow, that's what you want. He's right, but you have to study his paintings carefully to know how right he is.

When I first started favouring Bessie's, my demands never went beyond a coffee and sandwich or, maybe, a beer, so that I sometimes thought it a wonder that I wasn't asked to move on. But Greek waiters rarely take so extreme, so inhospitable a measure. At that time I knew nothing of the café's history. Now I do. For in the mid -'90s we eventually did what for years we'd been meaning to do. We took out a long-term rent on a small flat some fifteen minutes' walk down the coast from the port town, and we're there as often as we can manage and for sure never less than two months in each year. We've therefore come to know well native Greeks as well as a shifting population of incomers and ex-pats, among whom are the to-be-expected share of small-time crooks dodging British justice (thieves, property speculators, pornographers, drug-runners), and pseuds who find it possible to convince themselves and each other that they are genuine painters and/or writers. (Poets, naturally, for who would be at the trouble of writing prose.) Our flat is behind a hotel in the little village of Faros, which means 'lighthouse'. Needless to say there is no lighthouse, just as there are no partridges at Perdika (they've long since been shot), although there is a small harbour. This occupies more or less the same site as an ancient one, dating back to the fourth century BC, of which hardly a trace now remains.

I know about this, as I know about so much else to do with the island, from my friend Gerald Thompson. Gerald, who is now in his late seventies and who looks like a cheerful version of Samuel Beckett – same shock of white hair, piercing blue eyes and high beaked nose, but usually to be found smiling – is a former classics teacher from Hull who came to live permanently on the island in the early '80s, following what he calls 'a crude application of Thatcherite economics' to education. In other words, his school closed down its classics teaching, leaving Gerald without employment. For the previous twenty or so years he had brought boys to Aegina during the summer break in order to improve their modern Greek and to study Greek culture first hand, and like so many before and since he fell in love with the place. The loss of his teaching post gave him the chance to sell up and move to Aegina, where he built a house in the middle of the island and, you might say, began to put down roots, although the cliché is singularly inappropriate for so energetic, not to say tireless, a man. Soon he was walking all over the island, and taking especial delight in the side furthest away from the port town, where there are forests, craggy hills, and sudden, steep valleys. He followed ancient hunters' paths, (not to be confused with the paths made by those who tap pines for the resin that's an essential constituent of retsina – these paths take you into the forests all right but they lead you straight back to their starting point), he made paths of his own, and he also found the path which led men two thousand five hundred years ago from shore up to the sacred spot where the temple of Afaia was constructed. Out of his knowledge, he made a book he modestly calls *A Walker's Guide to Aegina*, which I published for him with some fine line drawings by Pauline, and in which he has much of interest to say about the island's history, modern as well as ancient.

It was Gerald who told me the history of Bessie's. It has its beginnings in New York. There, at the very end of the nineteenth century, a Greek immigrant, let's call him Yannis, read in his newspaper that a family of Greek extraction was looking for someone to accompany the coffin of a relative back to Greece for burial in native ground. Naturally, the successful applicant, in order to deal with local officials and their requirements, would have to speak good Greek and be conversant with Greek burial customs, and he could expect to be well paid for his work. He would also receive a free return steamship ticket to New York. Yannis applied, was accepted, and set sail with his unusual cargo. As the boat neared its destination, Yannis for some reason decided to take a peek inside the coffin. Surprise, surprise. There was no body. There was, however, a box which, when prised open, proved to contain gold bars and jewellery. By the time the ship docked at Piraeus the gold and jewels had become part of our man's property. He then made for Aegina, though why is not revealed, where he used the money to build a hotel in the middle of the island, conveniently near to the temple of Afaia, so that visitors who came from far and near to wander about the place would have somewhere to lay their weary bones. His mother, who was put in charge of the hotel, was called Bessie, and before long the hotel itself was called Bessie's. Unfortunately, the visitors did not come in sufficient numbers and after a few years the hotel was converted into a sanatorium for TB sufferers, to whom it could be recommended because of the clear, piney air, and because surrounding herds of goats guaranteed plentiful supplies of milk which was then held to be essential to the successful treatment of TB. But not wanting to give up on the hotel business, Yannis opened another establishment down on the waterfront, once more taking his mother's name – presumably to throw off the scent anyone from the outsmarted New York set who might have come looking for him.

As tall stories go, this is up with the best, but then the history of Aegina itself is, as I discovered in the early days when I began visiting it regularly, founded on improbable but powerful stories. One afternoon in late October, a hot, clear day with just enough of a breeze to make walking a pleasure, I had ambled away from Bessie's, past the church and Hotel Brown – now shut up for winter – and was following the coast road to what, although I didn't then know it, was Faros village, when I noticed a wide column of black ants crossing the path ahead of me and descending into a hole in the ground about a quarter of an inch across. As though riding an escalator down to the underworld, I thought. I was crouched over them, absorbed in their orderly disappearance, when an old woman passed. '*Myrmika,*' I thought she muttered. The word awoke associations, but with what? And then I remembered: the myrmidons, Achilles' soldiers who killed Hector.

Back in Athens, I consulted Harvey's *Oxford Companion to Classical Literature*. Myrmidons, it said, see under Aeacus. I turned to that entry and read, 'in Greek mythology son of Zeus and the nymph Aegina... He was a man of great piety, and when the inhabitants of his island, Aegina, were destroyed by a plague, Zeus, to reward him, created human beings out of ants (*myrmekes*) and these were called Myrmidons, the name by which the subjects of Peleus and Achilles are known in Homer.'

The *myrmekes* are endlessly visible. Not so the goddess Afaia, to whom one of the loveliest temples in the whole of Greece is dedicated. You can't any longer wander about it in as unimpeded a manner as I was able to do when I first went there in the autumn of 1984, and at the island's other major archaeological site, known locally as Kolona, visitors are also, and quite rightly, nowadays prevented from straying where they will.

Kolona: a single column on a high platform is all that remains of the temple built to Apollo in the fifth century BC. The ferry from Piraeus, as it nears Aegina, comes to the island port side on, then begins to follow the coast for several miles until, on a small, rocky headland, a white, broken column comes into view and you know that just beyond is journey's end, that the boat will soon begin a wide left-hand curve and that the town will suddenly be there: its biscuit-coloured customs house, the waterfront, and halfway along, almost opposite the fish market, the two caiques that sell fruit and vegetables; there will be the usual clutter of noises, smells, of bustle; one or two imperturbable men will, as always, squat on their haunches as they fish off the quayside, and, facing where the boats come in, you see the café Poseidon, where older men sit for hours at an end to 'take their coffee', while their wives drop off vast bags of produce before diving into the backstreets for further shopping, and the same waiter as ever moves unhurriedly from table to table, taking orders, consulting a coffee-drinker's newspaper for information about his favourite football team, discussing politics – *malakas* – and eyeing up the passing tourist trade. 'Please, here: we have fine food. You want breakfast?'

Kolona is always to be seen from the ferry. Not so Afaia. True, on the clearest of days, as the ferry passes the halfway point of its journey along Aegina's coast you can, if you look up to the rocky outline of far hills and then let your eye wander down their wooded flanks, sometimes just make out the spot where the temple stands, in a clearing below a cluster of tall, inexcusably ugly radio masts. But I do not believe the story that it forms one corner of a golden triangle of temples, the others being the Parthenon and Sounion, and that from any one of them you can see the other two. Given Athens's ever-present *nefos*, it would anyway be impossible to see the Parthenon from Afaia, or vice versa. But you can't see Sounion, either. It's too far along the mainland. Still, it's a good story.

The story of Afaia herself is suitably complicated. The maiden Afaia – the word meant invisible – was Cretan in origin, a friend of Artemis, and thus 'Britomartis', which Harvey says 'the epitomiser Solinus' took to mean 'sweet maid'. Having become the innocent cause of awakening King Minos's lust, she tried to escape him, tumbled into the sea, was rescued by some fishermen and carried to Aegina. However, once ashore, one of her rescuers 'offered her violence' – to quote the phrase by which an O Level crib of many years ago tried to skirt round Tarquin's intended rape of Lucrece – and in order to escape his advances she fled into the woods of Artemis and at once disappeared. I gather that over the centuries various visitors to the temple claim to have seen her, and indeed one hot August afternoon an Australian woman friend of ours glimpsed her. I never have, though I go to the temple often and never fail to be moved by its purity of outline, the massive and yet light-seeming Doric columns of local *poros* that stand clear against the blue sky, the combination of grandeur and acceptance of human scale that the temple celebrates rather than tries to oppress. It was built c. 490 BC, on the site of an older, square temple, and after long centuries of neglect and decay the site began to be excavated (for which read 'robbed') in the early nineteenth century by both British and German visitors. As a result, most of its treasures are now in Munich, though some have made their way to the National Museum in Athens, and a few are in the small on-site museum.

The Lenten period in Greece 1985 coincided with a month of indifferent weather. Before that began there had been Carnival, which as far as I could see involved women in dressing small children in not very interesting or flattering costumes with the occasional mask, and which culminated in Clean Monday, when it was the custom to go out and fly kites. Kite-flying symbolised the cleansing of the soul, and although I saw no kite-flyers in Athens, students of mine took themselves off to the various mountainsides around Athens for the occasion, and as I would later discover from a poem by Philip Ramp, the islanders made much of the day. They flew kites, they wandered across the island in various groups, they laughed, sang, dropped in at the houses of friends and at wayside tavernas, they ate, they got drunk.

In Athens, during the forty Lenten days, I kept my head down, worked on my book, taught, and went most nights to Babi's, whose Lenten food was especially delicious. You weren't supposed to eat meat during Lent. George joined me in choosing various vegetable dishes: lentils and mint with, I suppose, an egg to bind them, shaped into small balls and then quickly fried, courgettes boiled or – an especial favourite – sliced length-ways and fried with cheese, or, nearly as good, kneaded with lentils to form a patty, aubergines stuffed with aromatic rice, tomatoes ditto. After which, having bowed the knee to religious custom, George would tuck into a steak.

Early on Black Friday I caught the metro down to Piraeus. I was due that evening to meet George and others, but the day itself was free and I had a particular reason for spending it on Aegina. On my previous visit the friendly waiter at Bessie's had told me that Black Friday was a day of processions. 'People go from their churches through the streets. They carry the *epitaphios*, the body of Christ. Everyone will be there, and there will be bands to play and people to sing. Here, they do it, and all over the island, too. Many, many processions.'

'What time of day?'

'All day from the early afternoon.' I'd suggested to George that he come with me, but he refused. Watching the procession that would leave from his own local church – the one where Dimitris and Aleka had become man and wife – would be quite enough. George was a city man.

'And what time will that be?'

'Nine o'clock.'

That meant anytime before ten o'clock. On the other hand, the streets would, I knew, be crowded from early evening, as would all forms of transport.

'I'll be back,' I said.

On the ferry over, filled with excited couples and families going to the island for Easter, some men carrying whole carcasses of lamb (one woolly, bleating animal was tied to the underside of a bicycle cross-bar), others with kid goats prettily done up with pink ribbon, I thought how Greeks love the chance to take part in ceremony. Not flummery, but celebrating public and festive occasions. Flummery existed, but could be mocked. Once, on a wintry Sunday morning when I'd seen a friend off at Athens airport, I took the bus back to Syntagma Square. The square was filled with columns of soldiers, more or less in line, and waiting to begin some march or other that would presumably take them to the city's cathedral, just down from the square. At the head of one column stood an officer, puffed up with self-importance. With unwavering attention he gripped his drawn sword in what I assumed was the proper manner: vertically against his nose. Behind him, soldiers smoked and mocked his rigid stance. Then one crept forward, felt the edge of the officer's sword with his thumb and, to the laughter and applause of his mates, shook his head in a parody of disapproval. Imagine that in England? Impossible.

That had been at the very end of November. Earlier the same month, on the seventeenth, students and others took over the centre of Athens in order to commemorate the rising in 1973, the event which, though bloodily put down, signalled the beginning of the junta's end. All along Octobriou Street, site of the polytechnic and of the rising, loudspeakers were rigged from lampposts, and from early morning they disgorged music by Theodorakis and others, relayed speeches and poems, until, in mid-morning, a disorderly, good-humoured procession that had formed inside the polytechnic gates emerged and slowly trailed downtown for a rally in Syntagma Square. Ceremony in Greece seems often to require procession, no matter how apparently impromptu or casually organised. Would the Black Friday processions I was to witness be like that?

In the event, I saw only one. But there was much else to see.

Banners stretched across the waterfront wishing everyone KRONIA PASCHA, children posed beside kid goats tethered outside the butchers' shops, and the faces of people who wandered the streets, often pausing to greet old friends – a handshake here, kissing of cheeks there – were vivid with the sheer pleasure of being alive and in that place.

At Bessie's I asked someone when the processions would start.

'This evening.'

'But I was told they began much earlier.'

He shrugged and rocked his head back. Though he did not do this as emphatically as Manolis always managed when disagreeing with anything you said, the gesture all too clearly meant No. *Ochi*. Never.

I looked about for my friendly waiter, then remembered that he'd told me he would be going home for Easter – home being the island of Naxos.

Leaving Bessie's, I made my way along the crowded waterfront, then, drawn by the priestly chanting coming from the church's open doors, looked into Panaghitsa church. It was packed, mostly with women, all dressed in black and with black headscarves, although a number of men in black suits or black leather jackets and a shifting population of well-dressed children were also present. In the short time I watched, there were comings and goings, and through them the chanting went imperturbably on. But although a wooden pulpit, painted blue and white, had been set up on the far side of the road to face the church, its back to the corner of the waterfront, I could see no evidence of a likely procession.

I retraced my steps and at a waterfront *ouzerie* managed to find a table, one of those round, zinc-topped affairs scarcely large enough to hold a small plate of *mezes* and a glass of ouzo. The waiter here, a short man with a melon-sized stomach, confirmed my suspicions. There would definitely be no procession from any church before the evening. However, he added, there might be an afternoon procession from the town cemetery. Did I know where that was? I did, having passed it on a back lane leading away from port Aegina and down towards Faros village. But could I trust him? Mightn't it simply be better to cut my losses and head back to Athens? The other waiter had after all misled me. Not that I doubted his sincerity. He wanted me to see a procession, therefore he had told me there would be one. In fact, according to him there would be many processions, and I would be able to see most of them.

This would be neither the first nor last time that I was given information by people eager to help, which meant they told me whatever it was they assumed I wanted to hear. How far is the nearest bus stop, or café, or taverna, or hotel? Oh, just round the corner. Just round the corner might turn out to mean five miles away, and though I came to accept that this offered information was not maliciously intended, I was learning to be wary of it. I'd even drawn up a rule for measuring the reliability of such information: the more confidently it was offered, the less it was to be trusted. The rule worked pretty well.

But on this occasion my informant proved to be right. After lingering over a plate of salt sardines accompanied by black olives, slivers of hard-boiled egg and crouton-sized squares of hard salt cheese, all washed down with a couple of glasses of ouzo, I made my way to the cemetery. By the time I arrived a crowd was forming in the lane and, over the freshly-whitewashed walls, I could see others inside, among whom I recognised some of the town's shopkeepers and taverna owners.

The procession, when it began some twenty minutes later, wasn't much of an affair. Four men hoisted a small effigy of the dead Christ, enclosed in a glass box, onto their shoulders, a black-garbed priest followed, he in his turn was followed by the folk gathered inside the cemetery, and as they emerged into the lane they turned right and began to process away from town, followed by a group of children in white shirts and blouses, behind them men and women, all of them in black. Perhaps as many as a hundred made up the procession, certainly no more. There was some chanting, but of a band no sign. I decided against tagging along. It was the cemetery that drew my attention. I went through the arched entry, decorated for the occasion with branches of palm, and wandered about a space no larger than a hockey pitch, enclosed within whitewashed walls, and over which a cypress tree smoked up into the blue sky. The tombs, crowded together, had been most lovingly prepared for Easter, their marble scrubbed into gleaming whiteness or, more rarely, black. Wreaths of pink and white or blue and white flowers were draped over the crosses that stood at the head of most tombs, photographs of the dead were propped on their flat surfaces, behind, in many instances, vases of deftly-arranged flowers and small lit oil-lamps of coloured glass. In later years, when I regularly walked by the place at night, I would come to love the reassuring glow of these lamps, the feeling they gave of secret, unthreatening continuity, but for now what struck me was the way the little cemetery declared its belief in livingness.

There was nothing ostentatious, let alone insistent or unduly pious about this. It simply *was*. And then I remembered Seferis's remark to the effect that nobody can expect to understand Greece who fails to realise that for the Greeks the miraculous is a matter of fact. Over the years I have come to realise how piercingly true that remark is. Acceptance of the miraculous lies deep within the Greek psyche. So for example, on an occasion when Manos, Fotini, George, Pauline and I were going by ferry to Syros, we were joined below deck by an old woman who was journeying on to the next island of Tinos. This was in the middle of August, the time of year when, in 1922, a sailor had been led by a dream to discover an image of the Virgin high up in rock on the island. Every year since, therefore, people make an August pilgrimage to Tinos. The old woman was going, she told us, because the Virgin had appeared to her in a dream the previous night and instructed her to make the pilgrimage.

Just as our ferry turned to go into Syros the propeller caught on something, probably rock. There was a rasping sound, the boat shook for a moment, then continued its sweep into harbour. The old woman stood to disembark with us. 'Tinos is the next island,' Manos said, thinking she had mistaken her stop. But no.

'That propeller spoke with my dead husband's voice,' she said. 'He was warning me against believing my dreams. He wants me to go home at once.' And off she got.

Two years later, when Manos, Fotini, Pauline and I were returning from a week on Andros, we boarded a ferry crowded with gypsies who had been on their own pilgrimage to Tinos. Little girls, in long white or purple dresses with embroidered borders, gold at neck and ear, some with floral bands in their hair, ran giddily about the saloon where we sat, and one or two sprawled at length on the banquette seats, from which they were shooed by an indignant sailor on his way through the saloon. Fotini crossed herself anxiously, and the sailor, seeing this, winked at her, and showed her something in his open palm. 'Thanks God,' Fotini said, relaxing.

'What was all that about?' I asked.

'Gypsies can give you the evil eye,' Fotini said. 'It is bad to offend them. But the sailor showed me that he had a blue stone in his hand. That wards off the evil.'

At the time both Manos and Fotini were unbelievers, and Manos in particular was scathing about the church. But then, some years later, they became members of the Greek Orthodox community, which I suppose licenses their acceptance of the miraculous. In April 2004, the four of us visited Meteora in the north part of Thessaly. Here, giant plugs of rock shoot five or so hundred feet into the air, on top of each of them a monastery. (Question: how did the monks get up there in the seventh century, when the first monasteries were founded? Answer: on an eagle's back.) Manos, who was well-informed about the place, told me of an occasion in the Second World War when some German soldiers marched up, intending to massacre the monks of one of the monasteries, Agio Stephano. An old man stood in their way. 'Go back,' he told their officer. And the officer, struck by the old man's simple certainty, did as he was ordered. 'You see, the old man was St Stephen,' Manos said, adding that after the war the officer returned to the monastery and became a monk of the place.

I might have asked why the patron saints of the other monasteries didn't similarly manifest themselves and so save their occupants from the Nazis, but there would have been no point. Greeks are not only matter-of-fact believers in the miraculous, they are also fatalists. Why did Zeus help Achilles? Because he did. End of story. At that same visit to Meteora we were introduced to a partially-sighted monk, a sweet man who welcomed us with biscuits and coffee, and who explained that from boyhood he had devoted his life to the church. 'I was born blind,' he said, 'and at the age of seven my father brought me here to pray for the restoration of my sight. So I prayed, promising God that if he would give me my sight I would dedicate my life to him. And as I prayed I became aware of light coming into my right eye. I could see. It was a miracle. So what could I do but make good my promise?' As we left he gave me a piece of paper on which his name was printed, 'Father Ioannis', together with his telephone number. I have it still. Thessalia 489 60. 'Phone me if you would like me to pray for you,' he said.

It's easy to imagine miracles occurring at Meteora, that most miraculous of places. But they also happen on Aegina, as befits the island of the myrmidons and a disappearing goddess. I was told not long ago of several attempts to build a church on the outskirts of the port town, all of which came to nothing because the walls repeatedly fell down, and, no, it wasn't as a result of earth tremors or blasts from the quarrying (illegal, but it still goes on), nor even the fact that too much sand had been put in the mortar intended to bind the stones together. 'The workers would go away having finished a good day's work and when they came back next morning the walls had collapsed. But they found the reason. They were trying to build on the site of a pagan place, and this displeased the Virgin.'

I have heard different versions of this story. In one, a statue of the Virgin was found under the soil where the site of the church was proposed and the church could only be finished once the statue was rescued and put in the place of honour. In another, the site turned out to be where a massacre of Christians by Turks had occurred. The one thing all versions agree on is that attempts to build the church were repeatedly thwarted by other than human forces.

Do I believe in miracles? Of course not. Yet one Easter time, when my friend the poet Matt Simpson was staying with me on Aegina, we found ourselves sitting on the wall across from Hotel Brown gazing out to sea. 'Do you ever see dolphins here?' Matt asked. Had I been Greek, I would have answered 'Of course,' wanting him to hear what I assumed would most please him. But being English I said, truthfully, 'No. I've seen them further down the Saronic gulf, but here, never. They don't come this far.' They didn't, you see. But as I spoke three dolphins leapt from the sea about a hundred yards offshore, plunged back under, then leapt again; and so they went, leaping and plunging until they disappeared round the headland some way to our left.

After I left the cemetery I walked back to port, through thinner crowds – it was now late afternoon, siesta time still – and caught the next available ferry. It was virtually empty, though as we docked a massive queue was waiting to board for the return journey to Aegina. Throngs of people were everywhere. The metro seemed fuller than ever, and though many got out at Omonia – Athens' answer to Piccadilly Circus – just as many seemed to get on. Families, from the smallest of toddlers through to gnarled and arthritic grandmothers, packed into Victoria Square, and my stretch of Acharnon Street was lined with people waiting for the local procession. George and I somehow found each other and, pressed to the kerbside, waited with the rest.

Suddenly the crowd began to stir, people pushed forward, the air quickened with an excitement bordering on frenzy. 'They are coming,' George said. 'Of course it is not like it used to be. Once, there were brass bands, but not any longer.' As he spoke a rhythmic thud and oompah reached our ears. The air was pounding like a stethoscope. 'A brass band,' I said to George. He shrugged.

It took maybe twenty minutes for the procession to pass. There were boy scout troupes, girls in a blue and white uniform I couldn't recognise, men in soldier's gear, choirs, old Uncle Theo and all (in Greece 'Theo' is an affectionate term for older men, meaning 'uncle'), and, of course, the *epitaphios* itself, borne by four men and accompanied by priests and other church dignitaries. Many of those who marched, or rather shuffled along, carried candles which, in the gathering dark, gave the procession a kind of tremulous glamour. I thought of photographs I'd seen of mass Sunday School marches through rainy northern towns of England in the late nineteenth century, occasions from which, as far as the eye could tell, glamour was noticeably absent, though the children were dressed in Sunday best, and there, as here, the majority of the spectators were no doubt proud relatives and friends, as well as all who were forced onto the pavements by the fact that the pubs were shut.

Even here, in Athens, the cafés, bars and tavernas had temporarily closed, though some opened again later in the evening. Not Babi's, however. He and his brothers had gone back to their native village for Easter. Neither George nor I fancied going anywhere else so we agreed to call it a day and meet again for the Saturday night celebrations, which would begin shortly before midnight. Midnight was when Christ was declared risen.

Again, thousands were on the streets, thousands more crowded into the churches from which, as the bells began their mostly tuneless and painful clangour, they emerged, all of them holding lit tapers so that a river of light seemed to spill out of the church doors and puddle the surrounding streets, fireworks burst into the sky, showering red, blue and white stars, and youths raced through the crowds, letting off firecrackers. 'Every year people are killed by these bloody bastards,' George said. Then, 'Father has prepared some soup. Would you like to try it?'

The soup, of a kind served all over Greece at this time of year, was made from lambs' innards and its smell, warm, fatty, dark, permeated the entire apartment. Manolis welcomed us with the words 'Christos Anessi' (Christ is Risen), to which we had to reply, 'He is Indeed Risen'. Manolis pointed to a bowl of red-painted eggs, hard-boiled, and showed me how to grip one in order to smash its point against the one he held. His broke and I was instructed to try my egg against one George now held. George won. His mother, who didn't join in this ceremony, laughed with pleasure at his victory. We peeled the eggs, ate them and then the four of us got down to the business of drinking soup.

A little over twelve hours later I rejoined the Dandoulakis family for their Easter meal. This is probably the high point of the Greek calendar, and for once Manolis didn't cook the main dish. Instead, he had entrusted the lamb bought two days previously to a local bakehouse, from which we were to collect it shortly after noon. And at about that time – for once inattention to the clock was forbidden – George, Manolis and I set off through the streets, Manolis bustling ahead of us, in his outstretched arms a vast steel tray. The bakehouse, which seemed no larger than a store-room, was stiflingly hot, and the two men who worked there, their faces running in sweat, looked exhausted. They'd presumably been at it since early morning. A gathering of men, all with empty trays, were crammed into the tiny space, others stood outside on the pavement, plastic bottles of retsina were passed around, and we all took our turn to drink the health of those present. Our meat being at length declared ready, a good many crudely-hacked pieces of lamb were piled on the tray Manolis held out, together with a shovel-full of roast potatoes. As we marched back, Manolis stopping to invite passers-by to try a piece of hacked lamb, I thought of the fake medieval recipe that begins 'take one fair heron and hew it into gobbets'.

There were gobbets aplenty still on the tray when we reached home. There, we found the fish-bone-thin uncle I had met on previous occasions, Victoria's widowed sister, who looked very like her, though less anxious, and Manos and Fotini, elegant as ever, who had been bidden to the feast, and who, despite the difficulty of finding a taxi, had managed to arrive more or less on time, a matter on which I congratulated them.

This caused Manos some amusement. 'The English virtue,' he said.

'Well,' I said, 'Christ always rises on time.'

'Ah, but he is not English, he is Greek,' Manos said. And he then told me the joke about the five proofs of Christ's Greekness. Unpunctuality was not, however, one of them.

Towards the end of a long, convivial afternoon, and after we'd eaten as much as we possibly could of the various dishes set before us – spinach pies, tomatoes, sardines, cheese, salad, as well as the lamb – Fotini wanted to know whether I would care to join them for a meal on the following day.

'I'd love to,' I said, 'but I want to spend the day on Aegina.'

'That bloody island,' Manos said in mock despair. 'It's got its hooks into you. What is it this time?'

'Apparently there's some sort of festival up at Palaiachora,' I told them. 'People go there from all over the island, picnic, dance, make merry. Have you heard about it?'

But none of them had. Nor did they express any interest in joining me. So I went alone.

It's a most extraordinary place, Palaiachora. I read somewhere that it is reminiscent of Mistras, but having visited Mistras, that abandoned town near Sparta in the southern Peleponnese, I'm not sure the two places have much in common, beyond the fact that both are built on a rocky hillside. Mistras after all was an important city, first under the Franks, then Venetians, then the Turks, and it remained lived in and cared for until 1770, when, after it had been briefly liberated from Turkish control, the Albanians put it to the sword, then burnt it. The final devastation came in 1825, at the time of the Greek War of Independence, when the Egyptians completed the damage started by the Albanians. And yet many buildings, including some decidedly grand ones, still stand, and you can wander about the city streets, imagining what it must have been like in its heyday.

Not so Palaiachora. This is what Gerald tells us in his *Guide Book to Aegina*:

> During the 1000 years that the Mediterranean Sea was scourged by piratical depredations Palaiachora served the island as a capital and place of refuge. Hidden away in the hinterland, and yet commanding an extensive view of the surrounding seas, and protected on 3 sides by steep cliffs, it gave its inhabitants both ample warning of an impending attack and some defence against it. The proud fort with its deep dungeons which once crowned the hilltop, and likewise the countless humble dwellings that clustered the winding streets, have long since crumbled to ruins: but there survive some 26 chapels, many containing fine murals.

Spring is the best time for visiting this ruined place. Later in the year the vegetation has died back, but in April and May the hillside, unless there has been an unusually dry winter, is vivid with green, and thick with pointillist motifs of reds, yellows, blues, with flowers that seem to have jetted out of the earth and which, in the case of the aortal red of innumerable poppies, have a vibrancy that's augmented by the steady thrum of bees, busy about clover, lavender, rosemary, pink and white lilac. And the scents: rosemary, oregano, thyme, basil. You have only to step onto that hillside to know why the story of Persephone is bound to be a primal Greek myth and why her mother, Demeter, is, according to some philologists, the bearer of a name that means Mother Earth.

On the Easter Monday I first went to Palaiachora there were families dotted all about the hillside. Some had brought stringed instruments with them and sang; others sat or wandered about, noisy with good humour, still others visited the chapels that bore their names: Andreas, Dimitrius, Georgios... The hillside was glad with movement and sound. This was a celebration of life renewed, of promise that fruitfulness would come again and again, not merely through the agency of flowers and herbage, but through the small children who ran and tumbled, as vivid with life as the thick grass through which they waded, calling to each other or absorbed in their own play. I thought of how my students, who during the winter months became strangely sallow and increasingly melancholic, had, when I saw them a few days before Easter, become transformed by April sun, as though an inner switch had turned them from grave to gay, their skin in the same moment turned newly brown and glossy.

Years later, at the time of our visit to Meteora with Manos and Folini, I found myself staring at monastery murals depicting Christ, fresh from harrowing hell, as he waited to welcome the countless dead who, having burst up from underground, were about to step out onto the green earth. Who was that couple leading the way? Adam and Eve, Manos told me. Those who had brought death into the world were being welcomed back to life. They were being connected with, subsumed into, the story of Demeter and Persephone. I have no love for organised religion, but I might make an exception in the case of a religion so magnanimous, even exuberant, as that of the Greek church.

The Meeting on Acharnon Street

FOR GEORGE DANDOULAKIS

Into that teeming street plugged
to the city's heart I watched you
bustle from out the narrow lane where pain

for so long crowded our lives,
gutters I trawled for coins
to buy our daily bread, where mother's

other children ran away in blood,
and rumours of work hung thin as smoke
above the *kafeneion's* tavli tables.

Years that stumbled, their arms full of loss.

But now your step was eager, purposive,
so that my own pace quickened,
needing to keep your back in view. 'Father?'

In that unhindered light you turned.
Younger than when I saw you last, your eyes
welcomed my unasked question. 'I am

very happy now, my son,' you said, your
stubbled, carefree smile, bright-
ening, getting sweeter

as if you could not possibly be dead.

CHAPTER NINE

The May Election

IN THE EARLY SUMMER of 1985, after four years of rule by PASOK, the socialist party headed by Andreas Papandreou, Greece readied itself for a general election. Some of my Greek friends had their doubts about Papandreou: for all his charisma and despite his promises, was Greece that much better off since his coming to power four years previously? But George was impatient of such scepticism. His parents' lives had been transformed by PASOK. Before 1981, they had endured real financial hardship. Now, the state pension enabled them to live a decent life, admittedly in the 'home' that George paid for (Greeks typically make no distinction between apartment and house: *to spiti* is where they live, whether part of a building or the whole of it), but Manolis and Victoria could now buy food, clothes, and indulge in occasional luxuries that would formerly have been well beyond their reach.

In the weeks leading up to election day, George told me much about his parents and his own early life of which I'd been unaware. It wasn't so much that he was moved to confession as that the mere prospect of PASOK losing power – of which there was, so the opinion polls all agreed, precious little chance – goaded him into a furious contempt of anyone who slighted Papandreou's achievements, especially on behalf of the poor. And George's parents had been very poor. Manolis had fought in the Greek army but after demobilisation found work difficult to come by. He was trained in the garment industry but for all his skills, which included pattern-making – he showed me some delightful examples of island costume he had designed for stamping onto fabric – he was more often out of work than in. The reason for this, George explained, was that during the war his father had joined

the communist party. After 1945 he was therefore seen as potential trouble by the newly-installed 'loyalist' regime, and treated as a pariah.

I suspect that it's difficult if not impossible for anyone who isn't Greek to understand the hatred and suspicion that dominated social and professional life in those post-war years. Takis Sinopoulos, as mentioned in an earlier chapter, mourns the consequences of this hatred in his great poem, 'Deathfeast', where he talks of 'the black infection' that covered the map of Greece after 1944. It was an infection that wrecked families, divided communities, filled the prisons and the graveyards. It was as though some ancient curse, long buried in Greek soil, had once more risen to the surface and oozed its poison in every pore. Those who had fought against the Nazis were suddenly under suspicion, those who had collaborated were as suddenly *persona grata*. Decisions taken at Yalta, including the need for Greece to be part of the Western alliance, meant that any chance of the emergence of a Greek communist state had to be scotched. And this in its turn meant that many of those who had fought most ardently against the Germans now found themselves enemies of the state. It is impossible to know whether, left to itself, Greece might have become a communist nation. What is certain is that the Western alliance saw to it that those who, in their loathing of fascism, including the home-grown variety of the pre-war Metaxas dictatorship, did their damnedest to prevent Mussolini and then Hitler from succeeding, were after 1945 treated as though they were somehow traitors to the cause of liberation for which many of them had died.

The bitterness that resulted from this tragicomic turn of events ran and still runs deep. The Greek-Australian poet Dimitris Tsaloumas was born in 1921 on the island of Leros, at that time under Italian control. With the collapse of Mussolini's rule in 1943, the British briefly took over, but their control lasted for only three weeks. A numerically superior and better-equipped Nazi force was sent to the island and, after a short but bloody battle, regained control of Leros. Then, even before the final defeat of Hitler in 1945, back came the British. A time for rejoicing then? Well, no. In his full-length study of Tsaloumas, Con Caston has this to say:

'Those who were placed in power by the British ... were for the most part Royalists and men of the extreme right who had collaborated with the occupying forces [i.e. Italians and Germans] and who had scores to settle with their democratic opponents. The British military minions in Greece had seen to it that the infamous Security battalions, who had played the role of the Ukrainians in eastern Europe and the Vichy government in France, were incorporated into the newly established national army to fight EAM, the people's army. A great number of these characters ended up in the gendarmerie and arrived in the Dodocenese Islands to take over from the British. Thus was created an extreme cold war atmosphere of suspicion, spying, petty tyranny and revenge...'

In 1952 Dimitris Tsaloumas escaped to Australia, but from many conversations with him I know how the post-war treatment of those who had fought for democracy still rankles. They lost their jobs, some were imprisoned, others like him became virtual outcasts. During the war he had, he told me, carried papers hidden in his violin case from Leros to Rhodes and back again. (As an aspiring musician he was granted a certain freedom of movement.) These papers included messages from partisan groups, often giving precise information as to the disposition and movement of enemy troops, and the discovery of them would have led to his certain death. Fortunately, that never happened. Even more fortunately, soon after the war Lawrence Durrell, who was then writing his book on the Greek islands, visited Leros, and during his brief stay on the island – which he loathed – was sufficiently impressed by some poems Dimitris showed him to give the young man a note of introduction to Seferis, should Dimitris ever visit Athens. I gather the two met on at least one occasion, but of course Athens couldn't offer Dimitris escape from the stigma of his socialism. Australia, however, could.

But for many Greeks, including Manolis, there was no escape. George's father had to endure long years of unemployment. He and his wife, living in a basement flat in what was then an especially poor area of Athens near Acharnon Street, were frequently short of food, and it isn't perhaps surprising that, under such stress, Victoria suffered a number of miscarriages before George was born. Her mental health was severely affected by these experiences, and on at least one occasion she had to be hospitalised. As a boy George was frequently sent out to scour the streets of the neighbourhood, looking for quarter-drachm coins in order to buy bread. And in later years, when he was an adult and earning enough money to help his parents move to better accommodation, his mother refused, ever, to walk down the street where she had endured so much misery, would indeed take no matter how out-of-the-way a circuitous route in order to avoid it. When George told me this I thought of Dickens and the blacking factory, but whereas Dickens could only bring himself to reveal his secret shame, as he saw it, to his great friend, John Forster, George wanted people to know what his parents and thousands like them had suffered in the aftermath of war. The shame was not theirs. It belonged to those who, some of them denying their own collaborationist pasts, emerged as true-blue patriots determined to 'save' post-war Greece from socialism. As for the CIA-backed colonels, and their wish to 'put Greece into plaster', George could hardly contain his anger, nor his disdain for those who had supported them and who by their decision, or perhaps indecision, ensured the continued immiseration of so many of his countrymen.

By a quirk of coincidence, as I write these words on Thursday June 23rd, 2005, the Greek National Radio Service contacts me to tell me that the poet Manolis Anagnostakis has died. They want to know whether, as the publisher of the English translation of his poems, I will be prepared to say a few words about him. Yes, I say, I was proud to publish the work of so fine a poet who, let it not be forgotten, was very nearly silenced before he could write anything of note. For Anagnostakis, a communist who had fought for his country, was in 1945 imprisoned and within hours of being shot when he was unexpectedly reprieved. I could add that the far greater poet, Ritsos, was both then and later, under the colonels, sent to an island prison where he more than once came near death. But I don't, because as I speak my mind fills with memories of that other Manolis, George's father, who died two years ago, of his

instinctive courteousness, his generosity, his sudden rages but more habitual good cheer, above all, perhaps, that wonderful smile you felt you could hold your hands out to, it would so warm you. If Papandreou had done no more than guarantee long life to that smile, he deserved the people's vote.

But it goes without saying that he had done far more. Thanks to him, all forms of public transport were free before eight a.m. A symbolic gesture, perhaps, given that transport was anyway cheap enough, but one that was welcomed by thousands of working men and women. In addition, Papandreou had begun the setting up of hospitals on islands that hitherto had known only the most rudimentary forms of healthcare. He insisted that newly-qualified doctors, having been expensively educated by the state, and with generous salaries to look forward to, should spend time (three years, I think it was) working in the provinces before accepting posts in any of the major cities – effectively Kalamata, Patras, Thessoloniki and Athens. Oh, how they hated him for that. City Greeks typically have only contempt for their country cousins, and in any debate about country versus town they make plain which side they are on. (*A propos* of which I should note that my students could never see why William Morris claimed to be a utopian socialist: when I got some of them to read *News from Nowhere* they puzzled over his dislike of London, well-known, so they felt, to be a most sophisticated city. Fancy preferring the dull stupor of life upriver. They had a point. The doctors didn't.) Equally important, Papandreou greatly increased the numbers of students able to enter higher education. As with the doctors, so of course with many academics: they did their best to resist. Why should they be asked to teach the children of what they probably thought of as the lumpen proletariat? Some inevitably saw the opportunity to make more money ('My own anthology is available'). But for the most part they did little to help Papandreou's scheme. If necessity is the tyrant's plea, the academic's is invariably pressure of work ('I am a very busy man').

Students in the English department, almost to a person, were deeply cynical about what was on offer as the study of English literature, though they were far less condemnatory of the linguistics teaching. Almost all were first generation students. For the most part their parents had finished schooling at the age of fourteen; some had known scarcely any formal education, were, I suspect, functionally illiterate. Certainly my local supermarket contained a number of shoppers who would ask anyone, even me, to read out for them the prices on articles they wanted to buy. An old woman once explained that her eyesight wasn't sharp enough to distinguish the figures, but most of those who sought my help would simply thrust the article under my nose with the request '*poso kani?*' I imagine that when it came to voting they would place their cross beside the name they had worked hard to identify, although for all I know the ballot papers may have had logos accompanying the names. PASOK's was a rising sun, in green.

Voting was compulsory. That made sense. Everybody should be required to take an active part in the restored democracy. But then, of course, everyone in ancient Athenian democratic times did so. The Greeks, those people Dean Rusk announced were 'not yet ready for democracy', had invented it. In common with many other European nations, Greek elections were held on a Sunday, and as everyone was required to cast their votes in their birthplace, and as the government agreed to pick up the bill for all who had to journey any distance in order to vote, the election became a kind of jamboree.

All electioneering officially ended on Friday. By then, some of my students had already departed the scene. For them the election meant not merely doing their democratic duty but enjoying a brief holiday. Marianthi, who intended to vote for the Euro-communist party, left on the Thursday ferry for Rhodes, where her father was a boat-builder. Maria, an ardent supporter of PASOK, took the boat to Naxos. Angelika boarded a coach for Kalamata.

'Her father is New Democracy,' I was told. 'He hopes for the return of the monarchy.'

'Do many share his view?'

'Very few. Most royalists are in the Mani. But they will not prevail. Royalty in Greece is finished.' To emphasise the point, imaginary dust was brushed from open palms.

'We have a Greek royal,' I said. 'More German than Greek,' came the inevitable answer.

It was true. After the successful completion of the Greek war of liberation and independence in the early 1830s, a minor branch of Hapsburg monarchy was planted on the Greek throne. 'Still,' I said, 'most Brits think of him as Phil the Greek.'

A few years later, after the conservative administration in the UK had passed into law their obnoxious bill denying foreign men married to British women the automatic right to settle in the UK, I was able to send that particular anti-royalist friend the poet Gavin Ewart's two-liner on the subject:

> A thing of which we do not speak
> The queen is married to a Greek.

'And yet,' she replied, 'I have been listening to a commentator at Wimbledon,' – she was keen on tennis and watched it whenever she could – 'and he told us that "The cream of Europe is here today, including *King Constantine of Greece*." Why doesn't the bloody man know that he's the *Ex*-King!!!!!'

During his Friday night rally at Syntagma Square, Papandreou made a fleeting, contemptuous reference to the former royal family. It was greeted with laughter and applause. On the previous evening, I was told, Mitsotakis of New Democracy had steered clear of trouble by saying nothing of any plans to restore the monarchy, though there were rumours that some at least of his supporters were in favour of such a move. But they were far to the right of anywhere he dared to be. As for the Communists, they were of course republican and lost no chance to deride the former King. I'd gone to their Wednesday night rally out of curiosity, partly because several of my students were in one of the two versions of communism then existing in Greece (Euro and 'old' – i.e. Stalinist), and partly because I'd been told that communist rallies provided the best entertainment. The 'old' communists were rumoured to be the richest political party in Greece, owners of land and factories, and with filled coffers. They could therefore hand out food and drink in lavish amounts.

Not that night. The rally was well-attended but it by no means filled the square. The speeches were long, tedious, I understood very little, and most that I did seemed to consist of routine denunciations of capitalism, America and Western Liberalism. I think, though I can't be sure, the Pope also took a verbal battering. The applause was equally routine and looking around me I sensed that the appeal of communism was on the wane. The speakers and crowd were going through the motions, but it was clear that whatever visions had sustained them and their predecessors through the war and the terrible years that followed were now fading into near invisibility. The vision-as-hope with which Sinopoulos's 'Deathfeast' closes had been proved right:

> Light poured from the fruit-bearing sun
> In memory of the lost ones. So many years have passed
> I told them, our hair's turned gray.

> Little by little the voices died,
> Each face turned from me, one by one they left.
> They took to the valley, they dwindled into air.

> For the last time I gazed after them, called to them.
> The fire wasted to ash and through the window I saw

> How with just one star the night turns navigable

> How in an empty church the nameless dead
> Are lain among heaped flowers, are anointed.

Mitsotakis's Thursday night speech to his followers was accompanied by American-style razzmatazz, complete with cheerleaders, blaring music and hysterical, well-orchestrated applause from those packed into the square, many of whom, so I was told, had been bussed in for the occasion with the promise of some form of reward. Rent-a-crowd. I watched it all on television at George's, and while George jeered and swore spectacularly at the screen, the highlight of the evening undoubtedly came when Manolis heaved his bulk up from the chair on which he sprawled, slowly and laboriously turned, and then, bending, presented his vast bum to a close-up of Mitsotakis's face.

Dimitris, George and I planned to be in Syntagma Square for Friday's rally. In the event, however, we couldn't get near. The square was filled long before Papandreou appeared, as were most of the side roads leading into the square, and so, although loudspeakers relayed his words, we finally decided to beat a retreat. By now it was obvious that PASOK would easily win re-election. The mere promise to free the country of American air-bases was guarantee enough of that. Yet it wasn't so much the party people would vote for, it was Papandreou himself. PASOK was to all intents and purposes a one-man party and Papandreou, who had created it, was the people's hero. He had been imprisoned by the junta, had indeed come perilously near to being assassinated. (Only the intervention of LBJ, so it was rumoured, had saved his life.) From prison in Athens he had been whisked away to safety, but not before he had endured several beatings from Papadopoulos's police.

I can't any longer be sure how much in 1985 I knew about Papandreou's prison experiences. Something, certainly. But in the summer of 2003 I was asked to give a poetry reading at a summer school on Spetses. There, I discovered that the other reader was to be Nick Papandreou, the great man's younger son, who read from his semi-autobiographical novel, *Father Dancing*. Afterwards, over a meal, we talked about his boyhood recollections of the period leading up to the family's exile from Greece. He remembered in particular his American mother's nightly visits to the prison in which her husband was incarcerated, and how, though she wasn't allowed to see him, she would walk up and down the street outside puffing on a Pall Mall cigarette until an answering glow from a darkened cell-window where she knew he was housed told her that he was still alive. And in the novel itself, I read of how Nick and his older brother, Jason, were made, with other schoolchildren, to listen to civics lectures at which an army lieutenant instructed them in the new constitution and the 'restricted but expanded' rights of the citizen under the junta. Then, using an ancient map of Israel and Palestine, the lieutenant launched into a history lesson.

> 'Did you know that they used gypsy nails to crucify Christ?' he asked us. 'Did you know that the man who brought Jesus the vinegar sponge was black? Did you know it was Jews who stoned him?' The officer said that Judas, Herod, Plato, and the hippies in America were all linked to Communism and Socialism and to Greeks like our father.

Reading those words reminded me that Manos had told me of occasions when he had been among thousands of Athenian schoolchildren who were made to attend rallies at the old Olympic Stadium in order that they could be taught how to salute the Greek flag. And that in its turn brought yet again to mind the occasion when I had witnessed the ecstatic welcome given to Theodorakis and Ritsos at the National Theatre in the autumn of 1984. And *that* reminded me of another story I had been told, of how the colonels banned performances of *Prometheus Bound* because, early on in their dictatorship, when the play was staged in the great theatre of Dionysus below the Acropolis, at the point where Prometheus spurns Hermes's offer of reconciliation with the gods – 'I would rather suffer forever than be a slave such as you are' – the audience had broken into wild and prolonged applause.

Similar applause, or so I imagined, greeted Papandreou's words that Friday night in downtown Athens. And after all, why not? He had suffered for his democratic beliefs, had very nearly paid for them with his life. He had had the courage to oppose the American-protected murderous idiots who had done such damage to the nation. For that he had undergone years of exile. (I didn't then know that they were in fact pretty good years, during which he was fêted across Canada and North America, and that, although he was almost certainly kept under FBI surveillance, he endured no significant privations. Quite the opposite, in fact.) Now, in May 1985, his countrymen and women could openly rejoice in his triumph. Above all, though, you felt that it wasn't so much Papandreou they were celebrating as democratic Greece itself. That was the cause he had fought for and it was their cause too.

And yet, as we walked back uptown, away from the rally and its exalted air, George and Mitso, as George called Dimitris when he was feeling especially affectionate towards him, somehow contrived to lose the PASOK flags we had each been issued earlier in the evening as we marched down towards Syntagma. One minute they were holding them, the next, so it seemed, the flags had gone. But why?

'Because,' George said, 'it is safer that way.' And as we walked he explained that many generals under whom he worked at the Academy were not merely supporters of New Democracy, they none-too-secretly hankered after the good old days of the junta, when life had for them been sweet. Good money, privileges, power. 'And they still have ways of making life difficult for you if they suspect you are on the other side.'

'How?'

'Oh, they can make sure you do not get promotion. They can give you the worst timetable. They can spread lies, you know, perhaps arrange that your contract is cancelled. Pfft.' And he made an elaborate display of wiping his hands.

There seemed something close to paranoia about such fears. How, for goodness' sake, could any general even have known that George was carrying a PASOK flag? Did they have surveillance cameras pointed on the crowd in and around Syntagma Square?

But George was affronted by my scepticism. 'You must understand, they have spies everywhere. And informers.'

And then of course I remembered his story about how, when in the junta years he was doing his national service, he was made to spy on fellow soldiers, had been taught to steam open letters and report on any contents he found suspicious. Small wonder he thought the army was still a law unto itself.

But what of Dimitris? Why had he got rid of his PASOK flag? Ah, he said, he couldn't afford to be seen as a supporter of the socialists by customers who favoured New Democracy. 'They will take their custom elsewhere.'

'But what happens when one of your customers wants to talk politics and it becomes clear that he's in favour of New Democracy?'

'I agree with him, whatever he says. He is paying for my shop, for my food, for my children. I think to myself, OK, you are a bloody bastard, and I hope your wife is unfaithful to you. But I don't say nothing of what I think. It is better that way.'

That Friday evening was to be the last time I would eat at Babi's. The following day he and his brothers intended to go back to their village to vote. They would shut up Taverna ta Spata for the summer and work on the family farm. The taverna had no outside area and soon it would be too hot to eat inside. Babi would not open again until the autumn and by then I would be back in

England. That night, therefore, I called as many of my not-at-all-sad captains to me as was possible, and we had one more night's carouse. A mighty one it was, too. Several jugs of free retsina arrived at our table and at one point Babi produced a larger than usual wedge of Danish Blue cheese. 'For you, Mr John,' he said, 'a special gift.'

I have no love for that particular cheese, but it was important that I should eat it with every semblance of delight and I did so.

'You will come and see me again,' Babi said, as we stood to leave. I shook hands with him and his brothers.

'Next year,' I assured him, 'and the year after that. An annual pilgrimage to the best taverna in the world.'

He kissed me on both cheeks with more than usual gravity. 'I will expect you, then,' he said.

On Saturday evening a sizeable party of us went to a local cinema to see the film *Z*. Electioneering might be at an end, but Papandreou, a man of wiles if ever there was one, was too shrewd to miss a trick, and either he or one of his intimates had arranged that the film should be shown at various cinemas across the capital and, for all I know, throughout the whole of Greece. The queue we joined seemed a mile long, and though we all eventually gained admission, I doubt we should have been allowed entrance. At all events, the auditorium was full to overflowing, and we had to sit on the aisle steps of the balcony – others stood – while around us people of all ages smoked, drank, cheered and hissed as the film unfolded. *Z*, about the fraught times leading up to the junta years, is a clever and heartfelt satire on the mentality of those who yearn for the simple certainties of a police state, and it no doubt added an extra fillip to Papandreou's campaign, guaranteeing him a few more votes. My own attention was, however, diverted by and to the smokers who filled the auditorium and whose carelessly discarded cigarette stubs seemed calculated to set the place on fire. And if it does go up in flames, I thought, precious few of us will get out alive. Every safety exit was blocked, as far as I could make out in the murky, smoke-laden dark, all the aisles were crammed with seated bodies, and you couldn't see your way to the main doors for the intensity of the fug. It was scary and yet, as so often in Greece, I felt an exhilaration that rose above and even suppressed all other emotions.

Sunday, from early evening, I watched television with George, Manolis and Victoria as the election results began to come in. Some parts of the mainland were coloured New Democracy's blue, there were a few spots of red, but overall Greece was sprouting green. George was ecstatic, Manolis no less so. We toasted Papandreou's victory in good Greek brandy, after which we drank to the future.

'Down with Thatcher,' George shouted. Then, grinning, he added, 'You know how to free yourself of her?'

'Assassination?'

'By coming to live in Greece,' George said.

An Honest Trade

'Karagiosis ... is always on the look-out for the big deal
which will change his life.'
Aliki Bakoupoulo-Halls, *Modern Greek Theatre*

Today a tailor, he's inserting pins
in customers' svelte legs. That makes them hop.
When they kick out he mimes despair, then grins
and cartwheels backward, clean out of his shop.

Back on the street once more, it's just as well
he's tidy in his midwife's uniform.
These gun-strewn cops might slam him into jail
for ungentlemanly conduct – being born.

Should he try for a baker – men need bread,
and he could have them eat out of his hand.
Mercer, macer, magsman? Ach, he'll be dead
before he's learnt those trades, can understand

such classy skills. Meanwhile, his children starve –
or would do if he lacked the *nous* to tap
deep purses of those Rich Ones he makes laugh
a bit with his old flyblown, tumbling crap.

So off to bed to plot for next day's tricks,
not sure it makes good sense to be alive
but knowing that he'll kick against the pricks
all round. Winking, he tells us, 'I'll survive.'

CHAPTER TEN

Messene in July

L IKE SO MANY towns and villages in Greece, Mavromati, a small village in the southern Peleponnese, is a nondescript huddle of concrete and glass buildings, most of them erected in the past fifty or so years. Many have rusting steel rods thrusting up from their first or second-storey flat roofs, a sure sign that further storeys are or anyway were once planned; others seem no more than beginnings in raw brick with staircases that lead nowhere; still others look abandoned, their walls cracked and fissured, either by earth tremors or by poorly mixed concrete that sun and wind have found out. 'Greece is a building site,' a friend once said to me, and as with all building sites it is also a dumping ground for builders' materials that were surplus to need or that nobody has yet got around to using. More or less anywhere you go across the mainland or, for that matter, on the islands, even in remotest countryside miles from the nearest habitation, you are liable to stumble on bags of cement, piled up or strewn carelessly about, more often than not split open, their contents spreading a grey dust over vegetation, as well as straggling piles of bricks, coils of wire and the ubiquitous ferrous brown rods. Why should they be there? Is this a casual offloading? One more instance of the fly-tipping that infests the nation? Almost certainly. A building contract was completed, the builder ordered more than he needed, the customer paid, then got rid of it. Or perhaps someone had what he thought was a good idea for making some quick money by putting up houses on this particular spot, only to find that he couldn't get planning permission (though that is usually negotiable if you have enough of the folding stuff or are a friend or, better still, are or know a relation – 'cousin' – of the local mayor), or he belatedly came to realise that there was no chance of connecting electricity or running water. Well, never mind. That was last month's idea, this month we have a better one in a different place. Let's go.

The better idea may well involve opening a shop of some kind. 'Every Greek wants to own his own shop,' Manos told me, and Dimitris confirmed it. Far more than the English, the Greeks are a nation of shopkeepers. They haggle better, they put in longer hours, they make their customers welcome. And unlike the English, at least until recently, a Greek who acquired the lease or rent on a previously occupied shop tended to move in without making much alteration to the premises. Suppose a butcher takes over from an electrician. Instead of removing the electrician's sign, he simply adds his own. I've gone into more than one shop that claims to be a baker's *and* a laundry *and* a tobacconist's *and* an apothecary's. Stand on the pavement outside a typical small Greek shop and it isn't always clear from peering into the dimly-lit interior what the owner's line of business may be. So in you go, hoping, let's say, to buy some cigars, and find yourself confronted by an industrial-sized tumble dryer and heavy steam press. No

matter. '*Oriste,*' the man who's folding some newly-laundered sheets says. And he directs you to the nearest tobacconist, or – and I've known this – he takes you there himself, introduces you to the tobacconist and stands by making conversation while you complete your purchase, even shakes your hand as you say farewell. Alternatively – and I've experienced this, too, and on more than one occasion – the shop owner into whose place of business you've wrongly stepped sits you down on the chair which is a fixture of all shops, perhaps offers you a glass of ouzo, and then, when he's sure you're comfortably settled, goes to make the purchase for you.

It's wonderful and of course it makes good sense. After all, if you've gone into a laundry hoping for some cigars you might as easily go into a tobacconist's hoping he can dry-clean your trousers. Like the cheating by means of which my Greek students chose to help each other pass their examinations, this is co-operation, not competitiveness, and done with a clearly understandable purpose. I help you, you help me, together we will survive.

But we hadn't driven for miles through the lush green limestone country of the southern Peloponnese in order to try out the shops of Mavromati. We were here to look at the site of the ancient city of Messene, which lay some hundred feet below the modern village. By the time we arrived it was evening, and for the last few miles Yannis drove as fast as the road, twisting precipitously around steep, craggy hills, would allow. On or near the top of each of these hills were towers, 'castles', he said, many of them in a state of advanced decay. As we drove they'd appear first one side of the car, then the other, as though by magic they were leaping about the landscape. We were in outer Mani country, territory that neither the Turks nor the Nazis had been able fully to subdue, Yannis told us, and no wonder.

It was already late afternoon when we left his white-walled cottage, deep in an olive grove ringed by hills and near the small village called, as so many are, Skala, where the coach from Athens had dropped us some hours earlier. We were there at the suggestion of Fani, Yannis's partner. A friend of George's and like him a lecturer at the Military Academy, which was how we'd met earlier in the year, she now wanted to show us a part of mainland Greece we'd not otherwise have visited. Yannis, she explained, also taught in Athens, though he spent as much time as he could in the house his parents had bought for him, and was always delighted to play host to friends, his and hers. So, on a Sunday morning in mid-July, we joined her on a coach journey out through the dire suburbs of Athens spreading past Eleusis (no longer the site of sacred mysteries, it stank of the petrochemical industry that now dominated the skyline), stopping at modern, nondescript Corinth (which had to be entirely rebuilt after the devastating earthquake of 1922), Magalopolis (worse), and then, as the miles went by and the towns shrank into occasional outcrops of concrete and steel, the coach began to roll through a landscape of such primal beauty that it really did warrant the term Arcadian. Small rivers cutting between vividly green fields and olive groves among whose impossibly gnarled trunks you could make out flocks of sheep or goats, the thin clangour of their bells drifting through the coach's open windows along with scents of resinous pine, hay-dust, and the deep, sweet smell of sun-warmed earth. Two or three hours of such beauty, and then we were dropped off.

Country scents were all about us as we sat outside Yannis's cottage sipping beer, so, too, the strum of bees working the flowering grasses, jasmine and wild roses that clambered across his patio. Why move from this? But he wanted to show us Messene. And once we were in his car and heading for the site on which the ancient city stood, it turned out that he also wanted to show us some of his favourite spots along the way, including hillside springs from which water poured down and across the narrow roads along which we travelled, too fast I thought, but too slowly for his liking, at least if I could judge from the impatience with which he overtook the occasional car or tractor that meandered down the middle of some poorly-surfaced road.

At regular intervals, whenever we came to a wayside stream or spring, he would stop the car and make us get out and scoop up a handful of water. Though the sun beat down, the water was ice-cold. 'Taste it,' he said. 'Do you like?' Pauline nodded. 'Pure water. No contamination, it makes you feel good.' And he cupped his hands to throw water over his head and down the back of his neck. 'You do the same.' We did as he instructed and even before we were back in the car the sun had dried our skin.

On one occasion he stopped for no reason that we could see. 'This is an especial favourite,' Fani said as Pauline and I levered our way out of the cramped back seats of the sports car. We followed Yannis through a screen of tall reeds that fringed the road and found ourselves faced by a heap of limestone rock, hemmed in by bushes. Yannis circled the bushes, beckoning us to join him. There, hidden from view until you almost stepped into it, was a pool, no more than twelve feet across, formed by a deep, wide fissure in the rock. Not far below the surface of the brimming water small turtles moved slowly back and forth, fish, six or so inches long, flickering beneath them, and then, down past the fish, the water darkened into opacity. 'It is very deep,' Yannis said, 'I cannot reach the bottom.' He pulled his shirt over his head, handed it to Fotini, and dived in. We watched his body arrowing down, getting paler and more indistinct, until it disappeared into the dark. Like so many Greeks, Yannis was an expert swimmer and water was as much his natural element as it was that of the turtles, who, momentarily startled by the intrusion into their pool, now resumed their to-fro rowing, and then were again startled to the pool's sides as he finally reappeared, clasped an overhang of rock and hauled himself out.

'Artemis's bathing pool,' he said, gesturing to the bushes and sheltering rocks. 'I think this is a sacred place.' He shook his long hair vigorously, twisted it as though he were going to braid it, then took the shirt Fani handed to him, and a few moments later we were back in the car. 'We must make haste,' Fani said, and Yannis nodded.

But soon afterwards we stopped yet again, this time for an old woman, dressed from toe to top in black, a black veil thrown over her head, who sat immobile beside the narrow, now-rutted road, surrounded by gigantic watermelons. Further melons bulged from the panniers that hung on either side of the donkey which shared with her a fig tree's barely adequate shade. For some minutes Yannis chatted with her and then bought three of the biggest melons.

'We'll never eat them all,' Fani said, as she, Pauline and I sat with one each weighing down our laps.

'But they are cheap,' Yannis said, taking a bend on the wrong side of the road. 'Sixty drachms.'

Sixty drachms was, I reckoned, about twenty pence. Cheap indeed.

'And every drachm will go to her husband,' Fani said disapprovingly. 'Poor woman, she will have to take all the money she earns to the *kafeneion* where he'll be drinking and playing tavli with his friends, and the money she has worked for he will spend on more drink. I know him. He does no work and lives well.'

'It is the nature of marriage,' Yannis said, 'don't you agree, John? Women must work to keep their husbands in drink. When we are married, I will spend every night in the *kafeneion*. And every day, too, I will be spending your money.' He turned to Fani. 'But first I will lock you in the house, as a good husband should, to make certain that you receive no lover while I am out enjoying myself.'

'If I am locked in how will I be able to work for the money you say you need?' Fani asked, tweaking his ear.

'I'll think of something,' Yannis said.

As we drove into, then up and around, the increasingly steep hills, Yannis told us something about the history of the country we were passing through, Messenia, and its capital city. Originally called Ithone, the city had for some four hundred years from the seventh century BC been at war with its mightier neighbour, Sparta, which had regularly commandeered Messenian citizens to serve as slaves or helots. The Messenians had enjoyed one spectacular success when they aided the Athenians at the siege of Sphaktaria where, for the first time in their history, the Spartans found themselves having to surrender; but for the Messenians the victory was short-lived. Not long afterwards the Spartans came looking for them, their city was razed, its inhabitants killed, taken into slavery or scattered. Those who managed to get away were forced into exile. They sailed to Sicily where they founded the city of Messina. As for the original city, it slowly disappeared, went underground, and through the long, slow centuries was forgotten until, in 1895, an American archaeologist, Karl Blegen, began to dig on the site where the ancient Messene had once stood. Blegen was already famous for his discovery of Nestor's palace at Pilos, and his reputation was sufficient to ensure the necessary funds for his work at Messene. But after his death the money began to dry up; other sites seemed more promising or to hold out the hope of establishing a glittering reputation for those who dug there; and, Yannis concluded, 'nobody has been here to dig for many years. Messene is once more becoming a forgotten city. Very few people know about it, and hardly anyone visits the site.'

I was later to discover that Yannis wasn't always a reliable source of information. Once, when we were discussing Greek irregular verbs, or rather he was discussing while I listened, he told me that the reason the future tense of the verb to come, *tha iltha* – I will come – is different from the present tense, *erchoumai* – I come – is that it derives from the same root as the word for freedom, *elefteri*. 'And for Greeks,' Yannis said, his eyes glistening, 'freedom is always a state of becoming.' A nice idea, but, so Greek friends assure me, one entirely without etymological justification. About Messene, however, what he had to say was accurate enough, as I found when I read up more about the city's history. All he had neglected to mention was that, according to Pausanias, the fourth century BC Athenian general Epaminondas dreamt that he should build the Messenians a city to replace the old one 'on the slopes of Mt Ithome', a place sacred to them. Messengers were accordingly despatched to all parts to bid the Messenians return, which many did. The new city, whose outer walls apparently measured nine kilometres, took only eighty-five days to build, and those who built it 'worked with no other music but Boeotion and Argive pipes'. Then the Spartans came and knocked it down again.

We were getting near now. As Yannis talked, Pauline and I stared out of the car windows at the heat-struck countryside, the blend of tawny ochreous colours broken by an occasional twist of dark-green cypress, and by the olive leaves' silvery-grey undersides, immovable in the lingering heat. But the sky's blue was deepening towards violet, and I thought how easy it would be in a place like this to throw aside your archaeologist's trowel and do nothing but sit and drink in so much beauty. I remembered when, sitting with a friend over from England at a café terrace on the edge of Patras, and looking out onto the deep-blue waters of the Gulf of Corinth, with, for background, the mountains which included among their number a snow-capped Parnassus, he had suddenly said, 'A jug of retsina, some bread and olives, all this to look at, and why *shouldn't* you spend your life debating the meaning of beauty or whether men have souls?'

Another turn in the road and we came upon a sign: MAVROMATI. We'd finally arrived, and not a moment too soon, for it was now gone eight o'clock and there'd be little left to us of daylight. Yannis pulled up on the opposite side of the road from a *kafeneion*, a construction of regulation steel and glass, and seemingly deserted apart from an old woman standing at its entrance. Yannis waved to her, she waved back, grinned toothlessly, and then turned away.

In a grassy hollow below us was a small cemetery, surrounded as always in Greece by four-foot-high whitewashed walls and, in this instance, a cypress at each corner. With Yannis leading, we began to scramble down the steep, rutted track that curved towards the cemetery. Then, as we came nearer, bending low to avoid the overhanging branches of fig trees lining the way, we saw that the path went on round and past the cemetery walls. The earth here had a deep-baked smell, one, too, of almost fetid sweetness. 'Dungy earth,' I said aloud, but my words were lost in a sudden, frantic chirr of cicadas scouring the silence. And at that moment, too, bats were as suddenly flittering about our heads.

We turned a corner by a clump of dusty laurel bushes and nearly bumped into a small donkey which was plodding up the path towards us, bearing on its back an old man sat side-saddle. He and Yannis greeted each other warmly and exchanged some words.

'It's the custodian,' Fani explained, 'he's finished for the day.' And then, registering the distressed look on our faces, she added, 'Don't worry, it's an open site. We can go on and see what is there while the light lasts.'

Yannis turned to us. 'He will accompany us,' he said, as the man steered the donkey's head round and it began to plod back down the path. A few yards further downhill and the laurel bushes to our right opened to reveal a small field into which the donkey made its way. 'Not us,' Yannis said, 'we go on.' So on and down we went until the path swung left yet again.

'There it is,' Yannis said. And there it was.

There may be more beautiful sites scattered throughout Greece than the one we stood in front of that evening, and there are certainly grander ones. You could lose it in Olympia, or Delphi, or the sacred city at Dion. But that first encounter with ancient, all-but-lost Messene affected me more deeply than any other I have been to, more deeply even than the temple of Afaia, the hillside and bay of Asine, the open spaces of Troezen, the palace of Faestus. Not even Mycenae, which I'd visited on a misty day in February when the place seemed more than usually possessed of what anthropologists call 'mana', that spirit of impersonal, supernatural power, not even Mycenae spoke to me as Messene did. Only Epidaurus came close. I'd gone there the day after Manos, Fotini and I had been to Mycenae. As at Mycenae we had the place more or less to ourselves (a Japanese coach party came, took photos and within twenty minutes were gone again), and we spent hours wandering about the ruins of the Aesculaepian temple and outbuildings, Fotini, our expert guide, explaining about the stages in the healing process, how those brought to be cured were first of all immersed in one of the stone baths still evident, how afterwards they would retire to rest in the building that doubled as refectory and dormitory, and how, the next day, they would enter the odeon, place of music and song, and from there be taken to the tholus, the circular building at the very centre of the complex, where young women attended a priest who conducted sacred rites that remained forever mysterious. 'And after that,' Fotini said, 'the ill ones were cured.'

'Always?'

'Oh, yes,' Fotini said, very definitely, and who was I to argue?

Later on that same visit, we explored Epidaurus's vast amphitheatre, said to hold as many as twenty-eight thousand people, and while Manos and I, all alone, sat on the very top row, Fotini demonstrated the place's faultless acoustics by standing far below us, a remote figure on the open stage reciting in ancient Greek the opening lines of the *Iliad*. How could Messene hope to outdo that experience?

Perhaps it was the time of day, that magic moment when the earth tilts towards darkness but the light, still holding, gives an aura of soft clarity to every feature, which here included standing and fallen temple columns, pediments, walls and outlines of walls among which fig trees, cypress and laurel rooted. Perhaps it was that once again we had the place to ourselves. And there was also a sense that we were only just in time, were being given a tantalising glimpse of a lost place before it disappeared forever under the night sky.

You don't get dusk in Greece. One minute the sun is high above you. The next it has plunged below the earth. I once stood on the roof of my apartment block in Athens in order to time the sun's descent. Seven minutes. Imagine that and then imagine trying to explain to Greek students the powerful implication of the closing lines of Wordsworth's 'Ode to Immortality':

> The clouds that gather round the setting sun
> Do take a sober colouring from an eye
> That hath kept watch on man's mortality.

Or Gray's 'now fades the glimmering landscape'.

Don't Eskimos have thirty-one different words to describe snow? We ought to have more than we do for our northern experience of dying day. Dusk, twilight, owl-light, gloaming. Hardly enough. But this slow guttering of the light explains, or so I tell myself, why Greek melancholy is different from that of northern Europeans. Ours is compounded of feelings appropriate to lingering inevitability, of the slow encroachment of darkness and the anticipation of change. (That this day has been fine is no guarantee that tomorrow will be.) Forster once said that he was impressed by the fact that the typical illnesses of the north – cancer, tuberculosis – were slow to kill you; whereas in the Mediterranean countries a man could be fit in the morning and dead by nightfall. There's a figurative truth in this, perhaps, one which Forster links to what he regards as England's besetting mental and moral ills: hypocrisy and what he calls the undeveloped heart.

But I see it differently. Northern melancholy is characterised by regret or the acceptance of unattainable desires: hoping it might be so while knowing that it won't be. It's the tone of Tennyson's 'Tithonus', of 'after many a summer dies the swan', where 'summer' doesn't suggest a time of heat and joy but is a synecdoche for time passing. It's the tone, too, of Owen's 'And each slow dusk a drawing down of blinds'. Blinds used to be drawn in any house where someone lay dead. Owen is mourning soldiers killed before their time in France, but the dusk naturalises those deaths, makes them part of an inevitable process. It's this, of course, which explains why some readers have always felt uneasy with the line: too much pity, not enough anger.

Anger, sudden, hot anger, seems intrinsic to the Greek

temperament. It erupts and then drains away as quickly and thoroughly as that black mood into which I have known many a Greek man to suddenly drop, and from which he will as suddenly emerge. Dimitri the laundryman could and often did fall headlong into a pit of inexplicable despair, and it could happen at any time. A group of us might be eating at a favourite taverna, Dimitri keeping everyone, including the tables all around, entertained with mad jokes, anecdotes and antics. Then suddenly, like a lift whose power has been lost, he'd plummet into incommunicable silence. There was no point in trying to lift him out of his mood. But something would happen, a stray remark, a sighting – once it was a snail that poked its head out of its shell as George was set to eat it – there'd be a howl of laughter and Dimitri would be back above ground.

But now it was nine o'clock of an evening in mid-July, and we stood in a natural hollow under a steep bank some hundred or so feet above which the few lights of Mavromati were glowing lemon-yellow in the velvet air. The sun had fallen out of sight and to the west the sky, low down, was a saffron colour, above that rose-red, and then indigo darkening into a tidal sweep of black out of which, though the cicadas had slowed to silence, bats still wheeled and cavorted. The site's custodian, Nikos as we now knew his name to be, and tiny beside Yannis's muscular height, was busily gesturing to the few standing and more fallen columns as he talked, and Yannis translated for our benefit. Truth to tell, however, I took in very little of what either of them said. Something about the circumference of the city walls, the outline of which we could see curving away from us in both directions; something about the temples and the lavish decorations which would have been originally applied to them; something, too, about the recent discovery, a field away, of the top tiers of what was evidently a sizeable amphitheatre, although without a government grant there was little chance of further excavation.

While they talked, I wandered among the grassy ruins.

> We build with what we deem eternal rock,
> A distant age asks where the fabric stood

William Cowper had written in *The Task*, English melancholy no doubt partly stirred by his contemporary Gibbon's mighty work on the decline and fall of the greatest of all empires, and partly by that late-eighteenth-century awareness of how, with the advent of what later generations would call the industrial and agricultural revolutions, the English town and landscapes were disappearing, being pulled down, grubbed up, ploughed under. But Messene, I realised, didn't exude or prompt any feeling of melancholy. True, it lacked the mana of Mycenae, but for that I was grateful. No mighty spectres here, no Lion Gate through which to usher the bloodily destructive powers of the House of Atreus. Messene's own violent history lay buried under the tawny declivities and laurel-thick spaces where we variously stood or roamed about as the last light went and stars now salted the sky. What Messene had was peace, a deep peace it held to itself without need of visitors to affirm it. Some lines of Keats's came into my head:

> Through the green evening quiet in the sun,
> Through buried paths where sleepy twilight dreams
> The summer time away.

Why those lines? After all, this place wasn't at all remarkable for the light that lingers in the west. Whatever the glow that hung over the earth at Messene, it certainly couldn't be called twilight. On the other hand, just about everything else in those lines felt to belong here, though I could also sense – chose to sense – an intimation of that thronged Greek past which so possessed Seferis, and from which came 'The King of Asine'. But Messene wasn't like Asine. For all the city's tragic history, what most took hold of me was an awareness of some measured, achieved calm for which the English word 'serene' seems a poor substitute.

I don't know how long we stayed on the site, perhaps no more than half an hour, but by the time we began to struggle up the steep path to the village, we had only starlight to guide us. Yannis suggested a beer at the *kafeneion*. Would Mr Nikos like to join us there? He would, but first he proposed to show us the museum. This, when we reached it, turned out to be a building the size of a large garage, standing at the roadside some fifty yards beyond where we had left our car. The custodian produced a bunch of keys from deep inside his trouser pocket and ushered us into the musty but thankfully cool museum.

Small as the place was, it was quite large enough to house the few bits and pieces that made up the collection. A broken shaft of column here, a fragment of statuary there. Whatever of value had been unearthed on the site was presumably now in the National Museum or more probably housed in some foreign city: London, New York, Berlin. The unimportant remains over which we briefly hovered had mostly been handed in by locals. When the museum opened, not many years earlier, the government explained that it was the people's duty to bring to the curator what they or their forebears might in former times have carted away from the site and installed in their own houses.

'And did people do as they were asked?'

Yannis passed on my question to the custodian and laughed at his reply. Then he held out his right hand, scratching at the palm. '*Lefta*,' he said. 'They got money for all they handed in. He says that much that was handed in was all of fifty years old. If that.'

And yet some some valuable pieces came to light. One old shepherd brought the torso of a goddess – probably Artemis – that had been in the family for as long as anyone could remember. Another trundled along the base of a column that had served as a kitchen seat, always reserved for the oldest male of the family. 'The man who delivered it told us that he remembered as a small boy his grandfather alone being allowed to sit on it, then, following the old man's death, his father took it over, and now he had it as of right.'

'So handing it in was something of a sacrifice?'

'He told us that with the money we paid him he would buy a new chair.'

'Ah, so he got something back.'

'But not a chair. He went straight from here to the *kafeneion*.'

'Which is where we should be heading,' Yannis said to general agreement.

A few minutes later we were sitting around a square metal table, under the spread branches of a huge plane tree. Had the space in front of the *kafeneion* been any larger it would have been called the village's Plateia, but it was too small for more than the three tables huddled close together, and as none were occupied when we arrived we were able to go through the customary Greek palaver, a kind of ritualised dither, as to which one we should choose to sit at. The *kafeneion* stood directly up against a natural wall of limestone that rose sheer into the night sky until it was lost in clouds of foliage. Water from a spring far above us splashed down and ran beneath the table at which we sat, keeping the air cool and sweet. Over a long course of time the water had hollowed out a shallow basin at the foot of the rock face, and in this tiny pool two ducks now squatted, preening their feathers and staring indifferently at a large black dog that lapped at the water around their feet.

Beers and a large plate of mezes – olives, sardines, slices of tomato, hard-boiled eggs, cheese and sausage – were manoeuvred onto the square table round which we had grouped ourselves. We clinked glasses, drank and pecked at the food while the custodian told us stories about his work. One tale in particular intrigued me. A German family came every summer to spend a month in the area. Each time they came they visited the site of Messene, each time they hoped to get into the museum, and each time they were disappointed. 'I was on my annual holiday, you see, and I was the only key-holder, so they could not gain entrance.' (This by the way is not untypical: for years I tried to gain admission to the museum attached to Aegina's temple of Apollo – the Kolona – and never succeeded. When I asked townspeople why the museum was always closed they either denied that it was, or told me to come back tomorrow or that I should have called in the previous day. No use saying that I had tried the day before and that the place had been very evidently closed. Such a statement would be met by a dismissive shrug. I had clearly called at the wrong hour. But which would be the right hour? Another shrug. Or, alternatively, I would be on the receiving end of an impassioned claim that the museum must be open because Kirios Georgios, he who sells nuts, had been heard to announce that he was there himself only the other day. Or perhaps the cousin of Kirios Pavlos, the butcher, worked there, and she knew.) As to the Germans, for five years they came to Messene and always the custodian was away, visiting his son at Volos; always they would inform the *kafeneion* owner of their sorrow at not being able to see inside the museum. The sixth summer, therefore, the custodian decided to take his holiday later, so that he could for once show the German visitors around the museum.

'And this time they did not come?' I said, anticipating the ironic twist to his story.

Oh, no,' he said, puzzled by my remark, 'they came and I showed them the museum.'

'Bravo,' Fani said.

It struck me then that Greek storytelling is different from the kind those of us influenced by a more modern narrative mode take for granted. It doesn't require ironic reversals, a twist in the plotting. Greek stories are chronicles: and then... and then... and then. And Greek conversation is a steady unfolding of events, even a table of facts. I once sat on the town beach of Molivos, on Lesbos, listening to one Greek man tell another what at first seemed a tale of great passion, even derring-do. His voice, his gestures, were declamatory, emphatic, veering between tragedy and comedic triumph. Listening more closely I realised he was describing to his friend a taverna where he had eaten the previous night. Every dish was itemised, praised or, more rarely, criticised, the price he paid and the amount he had drunk given in detail. The other man sat listening attentively and for the most part silently, although he permitted himself an occasional 'bravo'. He was not bored. His turn would come. 'And after they had left Circe's island...'

At one point Fani asked whether the custodian had a deputy, someone to whom he could leave the key to the museum while he was away from his duties, who could guide visitors round the remains of the ancient city. It appeared not. The village was dying. The young men moved away. There was little work to be found in the area. Not only that; there was no secondary school here. As a result, for both work and education the young had to move to the cities, and once there they seldom returned except for summer holidays or to visit the families they had left behind: the old, the sick, the infirm. Mavromati had no future.

As if to confirm his words, the old woman who had served us now came to join us at our table. Yes, everything Kirios Nikos said was true. The village was dying. Perhaps the promised renewal of archaeological activity would bring some new faces, but only for a while. After that work was finished Mavromati would once more be forgotten. It would disappear.

'Like Messene itself,' Fani said.

I looked around me. At the back of the *kafeneion* two old men now sat playing tavli, and a small girl hovered near them, watching but saying nothing. Occasionally her glance would wander to our table, but there was no flicker of curiosity or even interest in her look. Presumably the custodian regularly brought visitors to the site here for drink and conversation. His words, which ought to have been saddening, seemed to belong as much to the order of things as the deep peace that lay over the now moonlit landscape.

A little later, our glasses drained, we stood, said our farewells and shook hands with Kirios Nikos and the old woman. The three of us who had left Athens early that morning were beginning to feel the effects of our long day, and a two-hour drive lay ahead of us.

As we walked back to the car I felt something brush against my bare ankle. Bending down, I saw by the light of the moon what appeared to be a giant grasshopper, too big for a cicada. It crouched beside my foot, pulsing slightly in the dim light. I touched it and it bounded forward several inches, then stopped again. 'We call that "the horse of the gods",' Yannis said, as I once more touched the night creature, lightly, not to frighten it, but to move it out of harm's way. Again it leapt forward and this time disappeared from the road's verge in the direction of the path that led down to the village cemetery and, beyond, below, and lost now in darkness, the site of the ancient city.

'Going home,' Pauline said.

Gathering

Not far out from Aegina town's beach
a flotilla of bashed straw hats
bobs on the early morning Aegean.

But now suddenly
up they rise into blue
air and under them – look!
ageing women, in red, black, rugose swimsuits,
wading pumpkin breasts and bums
candidly ashore.
                        And now, tented
in mad, towelled decorum, they hop
and teeter into frocks
vast as their hilarity,
and all the while sibilants, squawks –

starlings babble as they quit the beach,
disperse slowly inland.

But at evening, when the men have gone
to rake the sea for silver or parade
sprucely at the *kafeneions'* tavli tables,
the women gather again on swept
doorsteps or dragged-into-the-lane chairs,
clucky as hens, their days'
chaff picked over to the click
of knitting needles that two
by two fall silent
as night eases in and the warm

hay-scented air settles them.

CHAPTER ELEVEN

The Octopus

I WAS SITTING on my balcony looking up the lane. At my back, no more than fifty yards away, was the sea in which, half an hour earlier, I'd swum my two hundred strokes out, then back, dived, lounged, and exchanged a few words in Greek with various old ladies in their hats. A few came down to the beach accompanied by spindle-shanked, withered-chested husbands, but mostly they came on their own. For them all, wading into the sea with a kind of purposeful gaiety, immersion was a means to continue the conversation. The sea was where they went to talk. Now, though, it was empty. At a quarter to three in the afternoon everyone climbed out, wrapped themselves in towels and, having waved farewell – 'until tomorrow' – left the narrow strip of beach, its stones softened by layers of dried sea grass, and made their slow way home to lunch and, after lunch, siesta.

If I'd turned my head to look down the lane I'd have seen, beyond the narrow road that followed the coast from the port town to the fishing village at our island's foot, the small harbour where men I knew (and others I didn't) kept their fishing boats, and then, on the far side of the harbour's rocky wall, the sea, not the pale, translucent blue of morning, but a sheet of ruckled silver foil glittering under a sun hoisted to its highest point and covering the island in pure, sharp-shadowed heat.

Later in the afternoon the gulf's waters would turn back to a deep blue, then purple, then a strange, iridescent charcoal gray, and finally, just as the sun, larger now and blood-red, slid steeply below the mainland's rocky hills, the sea would become a flamey orange-crimson. It always did.

And at three p.m. I was, as always, on my balcony and looking up the lane to where bougainvillea spilled off roofs, over fences and walls, the white and violet-magenta flowers adding depth to the sky's flawless cobalt blue. I'd prepared and eaten my usual meal – sliced tomato, cucumber peeled and cut into quarter pieces, thin rings of green pepper, a wedge of feta cheese and a handful of the island's black olives, small, bitter, but surprisingly fleshy, olive oil poured over a sprinkling of oregano – which, together with a small loaf of fresh, crusty bread and several glasses of retsina, was making me heavy-headed under the afternoon's still heat. The heat was getting to the cicadas, too. What had sounded like the manic, high-speed grinding of coffee beans had by this time slowed to gravel sloshing round in a water-filled bag. Then the cicadas stopped altogether and there were no sounds at all. It was as though the island was holding its breath.

In the sudden, unaccustomed silence, bougainvillea flowers began to shake in a breeze I couldn't feel. From behind me came a deep, rumbling noise, like some piece of earth-moving equipment moving vastly up the lane, and then, as the balcony shook with increasing violence, Pavlos sprinted out of his basement flat below. 'Out,' he shouted, 'out, out.'

I got off the balcony as fast as I could, blundered through the flat and out of the front door, down the steps, through the gate he'd for once left open, and joined him in the lane.

The rumbling stopped, the earth was no longer shaking.

I looked round but we were alone. It was early September and most of those who lived along our lane were summer visitors who'd already said their goodbyes, bolted the shutters of their holiday houses, and gone back to their lives in Athens.

I don't know how long the two of us stood there in the lane, staring first away and then at each other in careful non-embarrassment, but it couldn't have been more than a few minutes at most. After which the cicadas began to ratchet up their noise and Pavlos let out a deep breath and smiled.

He was a handsome man, Pavlos. In earlier years, so I'd heard, he'd played as a professional for one of Greece's top football clubs – Panathanaikos had been mentioned – and though he was now in his fifties and his hair had turned silver-grey, he kept himself in good shape. There wasn't a nanogram of fat on his body. If it hadn't been for his slightly bowed legs he'd have looked the very image of the Poseidon I'd seen on countless occasions during visits to the National Archaeology Museum in Athens. Some time in the 1920s a fisherman had inadvertently raised the sea-god from the bottom of the eastern Aegean where he'd lain for over two thousand years. As that fisherman hauled on his net, exulting no doubt in its weight, he must have felt he was drawing up a prize catch. And in a way he was. Slightly larger than life-size, Poseidon stands on his plinth, naked, his perfectly muscled torso poised on long, slender legs a stride apart in order to balance arms that are raised in the act of hurling his trident. He has that profile you still occasionally see in Greek men and women and which is always called 'classical': nose parallel to the forehead's slant, ideally-proportioned chin in exact alignment with both. Pavlos, in his dark-blue singlet and shorts, and with his arm outstretched, palm upward to indicate the building we'd just left, was, above the waist at least, a sea-god.

'You see, Mr John,' he said proudly. 'You see. My building is built good. It don't fall down.'

It was as though he'd arranged the earthquake just for my benefit, in order to prove the strength of his house's foundations.

That evening at Tassos's waterfront taverna the talk was all of the earthquake. Four of us sat round the table I usually occupied – I chose it because it looked directly out at the harbour – offering each other bits of news, rumours, reports from the mainland. Dimitris, Spiros and Costas all made their living from the sea, although only Costas was called the fisherman. He was called that to distinguish him from Costas the potter. Costas the potter lived in a village up in the hills and he rarely came down to Tassos's taverna, but if you wanted to tell someone else about either man you had to make sure to distinguish them. You couldn't say 'I saw Costas this morning and he was complaining about his water bill,' or 'Costas's wife was down at the port in a new coat,' because you'd be told that he didn't or she hadn't been. To set matters right you had then to explain you meant Costas the fisherman, even if it was Costas the potter or his wife you'd met. 'Oh, Costas the fisherman, that's different. Yes, yes, I know.'

So Costas was the fisherman and Spiros was his cousin, a man about the same age as Costas as far as I could tell, in his forties, part of a three-man crew, whereas Costas had a half-share in a boat with someone called, I think, Georgios. As for Dimitris, or Mitsos as he was known, he was younger than the others, still in his twenties and not yet married. His father had been lost at sea when Mitsos was a boy and now he fished on his own, going out in a small boat on the stretch of water between our island and the mainland we could still just see, looming craggily into the night, along its foreshore an abacus of house lights.

None of us knew whether that part of the mainland had suffered, not even Tassos. As he handed me the moussaka I'd ordered, I asked him if he'd heard any news about the port town of Epidaurus, of Epidaurus itself, of Nafplion, and he jerked back his head. 'Nothing,' he said. 'But I think that is good news. I think it means they had good luck. Like us.'

We had indeed been lucky. The temblor had shaken many buildings on the island but from all accounts none had suffered more than superficial damage. In Athens, however, and especially at the earthquake's epicentre to the north of the city, the damage had been great. At least two factories had collapsed, burying nobody-knew-how-many workers; whole streets of apartment blocks were now unsafe; fifty people were already known to be dead, killed by falling masonry or crushed inside their own homes – the number was sure to rise; and thousands would be forced to sleep out.

'Yet Athens is built on rock,' Spiros said.

'Not where the quake was worst. Besides, those factories were no good.'

'How do you know?'

'I know,' Costas said.

Dimitris crossed himself. 'Thanks God, Corinth was spared,' he said.

Years earlier there had been a major earthquake centred on Corinth. It destroyed much of the city and killed many hundreds.

Costas the fisherman poured himself more retsina. 'That was indeed a terrible earthquake,' he said, shaking his head as though in disbelief at his own memories. There was a pause. 'Terrible,' he repeated. 'You know, Mr John, it ran all the way down to Hydra, all the way.' A further pause. We watched in silence as he broke a piece of bread and pushed it round his plate, then stuffed the crust into his mouth and began to chew.

'It was because of the earthquake that the octopus nearly drowned us,' he said.

'Ah, the octopus.' Tassos, arriving with another copper jug of retsina, rested a hand on Costas's shoulder. Tall, a full apron spread around his belly and over his white, short-sleeved shirt from which bulged massive biceps, he looked more like a professional wrestler than the even-tempered, generous-to-a-fault taverna owner he in fact was. 'I should have liked some of that octopus,' he said, and looked at me. 'On that octopus I could have fed my customers for a whole year. More, perhaps.'

'The biggest octopus in the world,' Spiros told me.

'Bigger.'

'Bigger than the biggest octopus in the world?'

Tassos looked unblinkingly at me. 'Bigger,' he said and turned away.

'Bless your mouth,' Costas said to the taverna owner's retreating back.

Spiros handed Costas a cigarette. 'You should tell Mr John about it,' he said, nodding in my direction. 'He hasn't heard the story. Have you?'

'It must have happened before I came to the island,' I said, pouring retsina for us all.

'It happened twenty years ago,' Costas said.

'Twenty-five!' Dimitris was insistent.

'Hey!' Spiros put a finger to his lips. 'You don't know when this thing happened, Mitsos, that long ago you were still at your mother's titty.'

'Twenty years ago,' Costas repeated. He stared hard at the table which was littered with the remains of our meal, strands of bottle-green spinach floating in lemony oil at the bottom of one plate, small golden finger-stalls of calamari on another, beside it a bowl of potato chips someone had ordered and then forgotten to eat. Then Costas shook his head, as though sorting his memories into shape. 'I had in that year a boat called the *Agia Anna*,' he said, raising his eyes to mine. 'A good boat, not as good as the *Alexandros*, but good, you understand. *Anna* is a safe boat, well-built, and one you can trust, no matter how hard blows the wind. We were three in that boat, my father, my brother Andreas, and me, the only one still alive.' And he crossed himself. 'In that boat we went everywhere around the Saronic islands, there was no fishing place we didn't know, nowhere we couldn't find the fish we wanted. Especially Hydra. There is sea off Hydra, Spiros knows it, where the gulf is very, very deep, good for mullet.' He lifted his glass and drank. 'So. There comes a day when father says we should fish for mullet.' Again he paused, reached for his cigarettes, took one and turned to Spiros. His cousin took out his lighter and Costas bent to its flame. As he straightened up he nodded at Spiros, drew smoke deeply into his chest and let it slowly trickle out through his nostrils. 'And that,' he said, 'was where we were, under the stars in that deep place when comes SUDDENLY the earthquake.' As he spoke the last words he crashed his fist down onto the table, making the tooth mugs of wine jump in their places.

Instinctively I put out a hand to steady mine and as I did so Tassos's arm reached over my shoulder with yet another jug of retsina. Costas nodded to me. I poured for him and then the rest of us.

'This earthquake,' Costas said, 'it comes so sudden we don't have time for anything, we are like a cork.' He looked into his glass and shuddered at what he seemed to see there, before wiping his full gray moustache with the back of his hand.

'And how do you know it is the earthquake that does this to you?' Spiros prompted him.

Costas looked round the table and made an undulating motion with his hand. 'Waves' he said. 'Not wind, not meltemi, you understand, but big, big waves. And where they come from? They come up through the sea. I tell you, without a good boat then you die. You go down,' and he plunged his hand beneath the table to indicate the way you'd die.

'And did other boats go under?' I asked.

'Many,' Costas said, looking first at Spiros, then Dimitris, who both nodded agreement, then across at me. 'So I heard. But not the *Agia Anna*. Not our boat.' And again he crossed himself. 'But we think, we must get away from here, in case there come the even bigger waves. Father tells us to steer for Hydra port. But first we must haul in our net.'

Spiros leant forward, chin resting on his cupped hand.

Costas bunched his fists, one above the other, his arms quivering with stalled energy. 'But the net don't come,' he said, and his voice was now no more than a whisper. 'It don't move.'

In the silence I heard Dimitris suck breath in through his clenched teeth.

'Then,' Costas said, raising his voice again, 'it *does* move. It begins to pull the boat along and then begins the boat to tip sideways, like so...' And he lurched over in his seat until his head was pressed against Spiros's arm.

'You mean something in the net was trying to capsize your boat? My God, that must have been terrifying. What did you do?'

Costas picked up one of Tassos's table knives and made deep, slashing motions with it. 'We cut the net away, like so. We lose our beautiful net, of course, but thanks God our lives we save. And then we can get into Hydra port.'

A further pause. I poured us all more retsina. 'And you're going to tell me that it was the octopus which did all that – got tangled in the net and tried to drag your boat under?'

Nobody spoke, although Spiros nodded.

'But how did you *know* it was an octopus? Did you *see* it? I mean, this all happened at night, didn't it?'

'Next morning,' Costas said, waving away my questions, 'a Hydra man, a ship's captain, tells us about the octopus. A fisherman, a friend of the captain's, knows all about it. For years this man go diving at the spot where we fish for mullet, and one time when he is down at the bottom he sees a cave and he is about to explore – you know – when he sees there is an eye at the entrance to the cave, looking at him, and this eye is as big as a cart wheel. So he comes up quick, back up to where he can breathe. Next time he goes diving he looks for the cave and there it is, and there the eye is also, looking out at him. And many, many times he dives and always is the eye and sometimes legs – how do you call them?'

'Tentacles,' I said.

'Tentacles, yes, tentacles showing. They are thick as tree trunks, the diver says, and as long.'

'The biggest octopus in the world,' Spiros said. 'Always there, always in its cave.'

'But if it didn't leave its cave how did it get into your net?'

'Ah.' Spiros wanted to explain but Costas silenced him with the

shake of his head. It was his story after all.

'Understand, Mr John,' he said, 'this earthquake that stretch from Corinth to Hydra is a very big, very strong earthquake. OK? So what does it do?' He looked at me, hard.

I shook my head. 'I don't know.'

'It shatters the cave where is the octopus, that is what it does. So now the octopus must get away. It has no home.'

'It was all at sea,' I said.

'You got it,' Costas said. He reached out his hand and shook mine.

In the silence, Costas looked at me, and perhaps he was smiling; Spiros was studying Costas's face, and Dimitris had turned away to watch a fishing-boat that was just chugging out from the safety of our harbour, steering for the sea that shone blackly under a tall, starlit sky.

I looked at my watch as Tassos returned with the bill and a final jug of retsina, this time only half filled. We were the last people in the taverna. I shared the wine between us and we banged our glasses on the table, then clinked them against each others'.

I took the bill from Tassos and got carefully to my feet. 'I'll pay,' I told the three fishermen, 'It'll be my contribution to the evening's entertainment.' And as they, too, stood and, having thanked me, began to drift away, Tassos folded the notes I handed him and pushed them down inside his apron pocket.

'Goodnight, Mr John,' he said. 'I wish you sweet dreams.'

The lane, as I walked slowly up it, was full of the honeyweight fragrance of jasmine, of small white flowers glimmering along Pavlos's railings.

Pavlos himself sat on the step outside his flat, looking up at the stars.

I closed the gate behind me and went and sat beside him.

'You have been at Tassos's,' Pavlos said, and he wasn't asking. 'You drink his retsina, you see stars bigger than any I can see.'

'I heard a big story, too,' I said, 'or a story about a big octopus.'

'Costas!' Pavlos laughed and swept his hand sideways in an open-fingered gesture of dismissal. 'The octopus from the cave that almost drowned him. I know, I know.' He put an arm round my shoulders. 'Costas,' he said, 'has a golden imagination.'

'It's all right', I said, 'I didn't think there was an octopus, but I liked hearing the story. He told it well.'

'There was no earthquake either – not anywhere near Hydra,' Pavlos said. 'There's been no earthquake there for over a hundred years.'

That did startle me. I thought of Spiros and Dimitris nodding agreement when Costas mentioned boats sent under by the sudden rush of waves. 'But all those boats that sank.'

Pavlos jerked his head back so violently I almost expected his neck to snap.

'Never,' he said, 'not one. Costas tells you that because he wants people to think his boats are safe to go in.' He turned to look at me. 'I have been told that his father and brother sank off Spetses in their so-safe boat.'

'The *Agia Anna*? You can't mean it.'

Pavlos shrugged. 'It's what I hear.'

'But is it true?'

He shrugged again. 'On this island people tell you many stories,' he said.

We sat looking up in silence at the stars. I shut one eye, then the other, making the stars shoot backwards and forwards across the night sky.

'But you know,' Pavlos finally said, 'you can trust what you see, even if what you hear is no good.' And as I levered myself up he patted the step on which I'd been sitting.

'Goodnight, Mr John,' he said, 'sleep safe.'

About the Author

John Lucas was born in Devon in 1937. He has taught English at universities throughout the world, and is Professor Emeritus at the Universities of Loughborough and Nottingham Trent. He has written and translated over forty books, including critical studies of Dickens, John Clare and Arnold Bennett, books on English poetry, as well as a life of his maternal grandfather, which combines biography with social history. In 2010 he published *Next Year Will be Better: A Memoir of England in the 1950s*.

His collections of poetry include *Studying Grosz on the Bus*, winner of Aldeburgh Festival Poetry Prize, *A World Perhaps: New & Selected Poems*, *Flute Music* and most recently, *Things to Say*. He has also edited an anthology, *The Isles of Greece*, for Eland. For over ten years he has been poetry reviewer for the New Statesman.

Lucas plays jazz cornet and trumpet with the Nottingham-based Burgundy Street Jazzmen. In 1994 he founded Shoestring Press.

Acknowledgements

Acknowledgements are due to the following journals where some of this material first appeared: *Island* (Australia), *The London Magazine*, *Penniless Press* and *Poetry Review*.

Acknowledgements are also due to Peterloo Poets for permission to reprint a number of poems from *Studying Grosz on the Bus* (1989) and to Sow's Ear Press/Trent Books for permission to reprint poems from *A World Perhaps: New and Selected Poems* (2002).

ELAND

61 Exmouth Market, London EC1R 4QL
Email: info@travelbooks.co.uk

Eland was started in 1982 to revive great travel books that had fallen out of print. Although the list has diversified into biography and fiction, it is united by a quest to define the spirit of place. These are books for travellers, and for readers who aspire to explore the world but who are also content to travel in their own minds. Eland books open out our understanding of other cultures, interpret the unknown and reveal different environments as well as celebrating the humour and occasional horrors of travel. We take immense trouble to select only the most readable books and therefore many readers collect the entire series.

All our books are printed on fine, pliable, cream-coloured paper. Most are still gathered in sections by our printer and sewn as well as glued, almost unheard of for a paperback book these days. This gives larger margins in the gutter, as well as making the books stronger.

There is a brief list of publications on the following pages, and extracts from each and every one of our books can be read on our website at www.travelbooks.co.uk. If you would like a free copy of our catalogue, please write or email (details above).